THE BOOK OF
ST MAWES
Pilots, Pilchards and Politics

CHRIS POLLARD

HALSGROVE

First published in Great Britain in 2007

British Library Cataloguing-in-Publication Data
A CIP record for this title is available from the British Library

ISBN 978 1 84114 631 7

HALSGROVE

Halsgrove House
Ryelands Industrial Estate
Bagley Green, Wellington
Somerset TA21 9PZ
T: 01823 653777
F: 01823 216796
Email: sales@halsgrove.com
Website: www.halsgrove.com

Frontispiece photograph: *St Mawes Harbour and Marine Parade*

Printed and bound in Great Britain by CPI Antony Rowe Ltd., Wiltshire

CONTENTS

Acknowledgments

Iwould like to thank everyone who has helped me to compile this book. Some of you have invited me into your homes and made me most welcome and told me things about my own family that I was unaware of. Some have lent me their precious photographs or told me their wonderful memories of old St Mawes. Some have gone out of their way to provide me with research which would have taken me a great deal longer to collect myself. Some have just chatted and told me the occasional story. To you all I am deeply indebted.

My thanks to Douglas Sawle, his cousin Charlie Collins and Charlie's daughter, Marilyn Skelton; Miles Carden and the St Mawes Sailing Club; Eileen and Jimmy Lelean; Val Bennett; Marilyn Morris; Tony Pawlyn and the National Maritime Museum at Falmouth; Janet Turner (née Gay); Douglas Clode; Pat Schichtar (née Clode); Marina Penhaligon (née Clode); Harry Harris; Cherry Ferris; Pip Garner; Jane Andain; Pam Royal, who taught at St Mawes School in the 1950s when she was Miss Smith; and my wife, Mary Alice Pollard, (www.justnicephotos.com) for her wonderful photos of modern-day St Mawes and for the countless hours she has put into this project. And although no longer with us, Megan and Butch Gay; Muriel Dotson; Donald Pollard; Cyril Johns; June January (née Tiddy) and Annie Pollard (née German), all of whom contributed to this book by never tiring of telling me of their love for St Mawes.

Author Chris Pollard with St Mawes Castle in the background.

Introduction

The story of St Mawes is indeed a fascinating one, and has been a great pleasure to compile. The village holds a great interest for me as my great-grandparents lived on the 'Ropewalk', my great-grandfather was one of the crew of No.10 pilot boat and my grandmother was the organist at the Congregational chapel for many years.

Set in its sheltered position, St Mawes has often been described as the jewel of the Roseland. But its almost Mediterranean appearance, although pleasing to the eye, cannot hold a candle to its history and to the families who made this small fishing village a place of great national importance. Its Castle was built by Henry VIII in 1542, and was at one time manned by up to 100 soldiers. In the 1500s St Mawes became a Borough Town, which gave it the right to send two members to Parliament. Its importance in the fishing, shipping, piloting and boatbuilding trades has seen St Mawes prosper through the years. Some members of the old families, however, decided to sail to distant shores in search of a better and more profitable life. Some of them returned to their birth-place having gained a much wider view of the world, while others never saw St Mawes again.

Long-time residents have seen the village expand way beyond its natural boundaries, where the cottages were huddled around the harbour. Now a magnet for holiday-makers, with its busy hotels, bars and sailing club, St Mawes still retains much of its old-world charm. A good number of the old families are still well represented, and this makes for a strong community spirit.

Watercolour, painted in St Mawes, 1893.

✦ CHAPTER 1 ✦

Early Christian Settlement

First mentioned in 1284, St Mawes was known by the Cornish name 'Lavada', or 'Lavousa', which implies an early Christian enclosure. First licensed in 1381, the chapel of St Mawes, with its cemetery and holy well, was in continuous use until Elizabethan times.

In other historical records, St Mawes is recorded as Saint Mary's. The historian Tonkin thought that it was '... called St. Mary's for that it was built upon the Priory lands of St Anthony, a cell of Plymouth St Mary's in Devon.'

In 1538 John Leyland was sent out '... into every shire' by King Henry VIII to make maps and records of all the king's lands. When he reached St Mawes in 1542 he wrote:

From St Just Pille or Creek to St Mauditus Creek is a mile dim. The Point of the land betwixt St Just Creal and St Maws is of sum caullid Pendinas, on this Poinl stondith as yn the entery of St Maws Creek a Castelle ofj Forteres late begon by the King.

On turning his attention to the village, he wrote:

Scant a quarter of a mile from the Castle on the same side upper into the land is a 'Praty Village or Fishcha Town with a Pere called St. Maws' and there is a Chapel of hymn and his Chair of stone a little without and his well.

It would appear that, like many other Cornish saints, Maudus came originally from Wales and settled here in the sixth century. When the holy man arrived in what we now call the parish of St Just, it was known as Corsult.

It is said that he was a good but strict teacher and that he formed a chair out of solid rock, where he passed the hours administering to the needs of the people. Legend says that the waters from the well of St Maudus were a sure cure for worms and other such complaints. After long periods of neglect, the well was repaired with a stone arch and carved oak doors designed by Mrs Pollard, and in 1939 it was rededicated by the Bishop of Truro.

According to another legend, which may have some foundation in fact, Breton raiders landed here and set fire to part of the village. Also, in an undated report, three crouched burials were found in an upright position on the high ground north-west of the castle. These were possibly victims of a plague, as St Just Pool was regularly used for quarantine purposes in times of epidemic.

The Holy Well, 2007.

St Mawes Castle, 2007.

✦ CHAPTER 2 ✦

St Mawes Castle

If there is a single thing in its history that changed the fortunes of the one-time 'Fischar Town' spoken of by Leyland, it was the building of the castle. This building changed St Mawes from a quiet backwater to a major place of defence, and saw the trade and population of the village increase considerably.

By 1620 there were '40 Pikemen, 40 soldiers armed with muskets and 20 with calivers'. All these men had to be accommodated, fed and provided for. It is recorded that, in 1636, many of the 100 men stationed there were living in or near the castle. No doubt a lot of their victuals were purchased locally.

Here the local fishermen would have found an ever-open market, as would the farmers who provided the garrison with meat and vegetables.

In 1641, when the Protestation Returns were compiled, there were 16 soldiers living in the Castle.

A promise vow and Protestation taken at his Majesty's Castle of St Mawes by Hanniball Bonython commanding there under the right Honourable Thomas of Arundell and Surrey Earle Marshall of England together by all the soldiers of the foresaid garrison whose names are here under written.

Ha Bonython	*John Stidston*
Richard Tremayne Porter	*Henry Clarke*
Henry Teage	*Tho Holman*
Henry Warren	*John Gidly*
James John	*Thomas Babbe*
Thomas Aundorowe	*Henrie Woulcock*
William Warren	*Peter Rawling*
Hugh Medlecott	*George Slee*

St Mawes Castle was built by order of King Henry VIII with money gained by the 'spoliation of the monasteries'. The king had already seen the destruction that the Spanish had caused at Penzance and this was further brought home by the sacking of Penryn by the French.

On receiving news of these atrocities in his kingdom, Henry is recorded as saying, 'I shall go to Cornwall myself and organise your defence; there is nothing more I can do than that.'

At this time, Henry was on honeymoon with his second wife, Ann Boleyn, and so the king and his new bride came to Cornwall by sea as, at that time and for several hundred years to come, there were no decent roads into the county.

Construction of the Castle, which was designed by German military architect Stephen, was finally begun in 1542, although it was not completed until the following year.

It is believed that much of the stone used in the building was brought across the river from the demolished Priory at St Anthony. It would appear that the Castle at St Mawes was completed before the one at Pendennis.

In the archives of the British Museum there is a chart, drawn up in the reign of King Henry VIII, on which Pendennis appears but its castle is not shown. The castle at St Mawes, however, is clearly marked and illustrated. This chart, drawn up in 1542, appears to predate Pendennis Castle by some 12 months. The superintendent of works at St Mawes was a Mr Trefrey, from Fowey.

There are various legends as to where King Henry and Ann Boleyn stayed on their visit to the Roseland. It is said they honeymooned at St Mawes Castle; this, of course, would have been extremely difficult, as it had not yet been built. Tolverne has also been given as the location. It is said that the happy couple stayed there for two nights and, on leaving, the king gave his name to the ferry crossing now known as the King Harry Ferry. They may well have stayed at Tolverne, as there was a substantial manor-house there at that time, but as for the king giving his name to the ferry crossing, this cannot be correct, as the crossing takes its name from the earlier King, Henry VI. There was at one time a chapel on the Philleigh side of the crossing dedicated to 'our lady and King Henry VI'.

A far more plausible claim is that they stayed at the Monastery of St Anthony, if it had not already been demolished. Here, in its little church, the coat of arms of Henry and Ann can be seen. This church is said to be the only one that Henry personally had restored. Also of interest is the field name of 'Pardon Bank', which is to be found at Trewince. Local tradition tells us that Henry VIII held court here and pardoned all political offenders in the area.

In 1544 Michael Vyvyan Esq. was appointed the first governor of St Mawes Castle, and on his death in July 1561 he was succeeded by his son, Hannibal. This prominent Cornish family would go on to provide governors for the castle for the next 150 years. The castle was strengthened in 1550 with 'two barbicans'.

By 1580 there were three companies of 100 men for Pendennis, St Mawes and St Michael's Mount. At this time, a new system was being instituted whereby, instead of training for two days twice a year, which, it was felt, did not keep the men at their peak, it was proposed that they be trained ten times a year by captains who would travel from one group to another.

On 31 October 1595 Hannibal wrote to Sir George Carew, who was the Lieutenant of Ordnance, complaining bitterly of the lack of proper armament:

The receipt of half a last of powder and a ton of shot, I return a brass cannon, a demi culverln and other iron ordnance as unserviceable and want a receipt. I gave my opinion as to what pieces I thought necessary for St Mawes Castle, where I will not dwell unless I have a better supply, vis a whole culverin, four demi culverins and three sakers, with some more muskets and powder.

It is recorded that Governor Hannibal Vyvyan was paid £118.12s.6d. annually.

The State Papers reveal that the upkeep of the Castle was a recurring problem and one that seems often to have received less attention than it deserved. By the time Hannibal died in 1603 and his son, Sir Francis Vivian (the spelling of their surname had changed), was appointed to the post, we find him asking for £700 for repairs. However, no money was received until 3 June 1628, when a payment of £253 was awarded.

By 1630 Hannibal Bonithon was Lieutenant Governor at St Mawes. Sir William Killigrew was then Captain of Pendennis Castle. In that year we find Sir William complaining that '... for the last two years, ships had been stayed and questioned at St Mawes Castle and this had been accustomed to be done at Pendennis Castle only.'

The Mayor of St Mawes wrote to the Admiralty and stated:

The Commander of the Castle there have required all shipping to make their repair to the Castle for 40 years and they have heard that the like course was used ever since the Castle was finished.

On the same day, a similar certificate was sent by the inhabitants of St Just, Philleigh and St Anthony.

In 1631 both St Mawes and Pendennis Castles opened fire on a privateer who had boldly sailed into the Fal in search of spoils. A year later, the former Governor, Sir Francis Vivian, was accused of 'not keeping the proper number of soldiers in his garrison and putting the money received for their wages into his own purse'. He was fined £200.

By 1636 there were 100 armed men living in and around the castle. Recorded in the State Papers, we find, 'St Mawes Castle; There is a company of 100 men near adjoining that are appointed to address themselves to ye Castle upon any occasion.'

In 1643 Major Bonithon also found himself in deep water with his superiors, when several soldiers in his command gave evidence against him at

Bodmin, and in January of the following year, these complaints were brought forward at the 'sessions of the peace' at Truro. The charges brought against him accused him of embezzling his soldiers' pay, smuggling tobacco and 'disaffection of the King's cause'.

The next day, Sir Richard Grenville wrote to the Prince of Wales and informed him of the facts, but, with the Civil War raging, nothing was done. When Major Bonithon received word that a treaty had been signed at Tresillian Bridge (as the hamlet was then known) which was to herald the end of the Civil War, he sent word to Sir Thomas Fairfax offering the surrender of St Mawes Castle.

Meanwhile, across the river at Pendennis, Col Arundel had no such thoughts in his mind and sent word to St Mawes offering Major Bonithon a 'safe haven'. Arundel was well aware that, under attack from the land, St Mawes would have been an easy target, with little chance of defending itself. Major Bonithon refused the invitation of his brother-in-arms and chose to seek favour with the Parliamentary forces. He no doubt felt that he had already lost a great deal of credibility with the king, on account of the charges brought against him.

In a letter dated 19 March 1644 and read in the House of Commons on 23 March, it was stated:

Every hour, more Gentlemen of quality doe come in. On this day Col Trevanion came from Penrin and some of his Officers came to Truro with their Colours flying and their men armed; even from the Lord Hoptons head quarters, which are now at Camborne. This hath wrought such operations upon the Governour at Saint Mawes that he hath sent to the General to be received into favour and will deliver up the Castle, Fort Ordnance, Arms and Ammunition; and accordingly there is forces sent away this night to take Possession thereof. Arundell the Governor of Pendennis sent to tempt the Governor at St Mawes to come in the Castle of Pendennis; He refused the same and as aforesaid craved the ayd of this Army. There are two great Brasse Pieces of Ordnance in the fort, of about 4000 weight a piece.

And so St Mawes Castle was surrendered to Sir Thomas Fairfax without a shot being fired. In his letter to the Commons, dated March 1646, Fairfax reports on the Tresillian Treaty, which he had signed with Sir Ralph Hopton (for the king), and stated:

The reputation of this hath already produced a surrender of Saint Mawes Castle; wherein we found about thirteen Guns and a good proportion of Ammunition; which place gives you a better interest in Falmouth Harbour, than the enemy hath; for by the advantage hereof you may bring in Shipping without hazard, which they cannot.

After the surrender of the castle on 13 March 1646, it

was without a governor until August, when Lieutenant-Colonel George Kekewich was appointed. The House of Commons papers state:

He hath been in the service of the State, in Plymouth, Cornwall and Devonshire, ever since the beginning of these troubles; and being reduced, he is out of any employment; therefore desires some place, where he may do the state further service; it is ordered that this House thinks it fit the Petitioner be made Governor of Saint Mawes Castle in Cornwall; and that the concurrence of the House of Commons be desired herein.

Parliament used the castle as a prison. Well-known Cornish loyalist Jonathan Rashleigh, of Menabilly, near Fowey, imprisoned there from February 1650 to May 1651, later claimed: 'I was being kept a prisoner in St Mawes Castle. It cost me £100.'

By 1660, Parliament had lost much of its former influence and, on the orders of King Charles II, Kekewich was replaced by Sir Richard Vivian, son of the former governor, Sir Francis.

The great days of St Mawes Castle were now over. The garrison was greatly reduced and we find Sir Richard writing to the king on 29 September 1660 asking for: 'A few more Soldiers to maintain the watch, for there is at present but one Gunner and twelve Soldiers here.'

Sir Richard died in 1665 and was succeeded by yet another Vivian, his son Sir Vyel. This gentleman was to be the last of the long line of Vivians at the castle. When he died childless in 1696 a name now familiar in St Mawes appeared on the scene.

Sir Joseph Tredenham was appointed governor but held his post for only two years before he was displaced by King William II and succeeded by Hugh Boscawen who, in 1720, became Lord Falmouth.

The year before Joseph Tredenham obtained his position at St Mawes Castle, he is recorded as the Lord of the manor of Tolverne and we find him in 1664 granting a lease of passage at Tolverne to Alexander Couch.

The lease included:

... the passage boat and passage money, half the fish taken in Tolverne Weir, the passage house and cellars, three fields, a mowhay and the right to land sand and dry nets, pasture for a horse and mare in Chapel Wood,

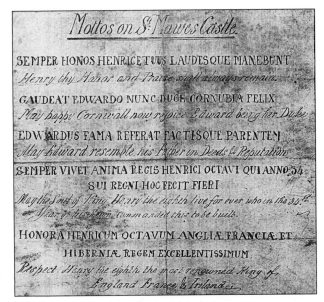

Mottos on St Mawes Castle.

the right to take water from the spring there and fuel of thorns, broom and furze from Polgurran Wood and Lower Burlase.

The rent was to be 26s.8d, and the Lord was to have free passage for his family and household.

On 1 December 1884 the *West Briton* stated that the Castle at St Mawes was manned by two gunners of the RA and that they received their pay weekly from Pendennis.

To convey it across to them the garrison boat, with six men and a coxswain, is employed, the men being paid 4d. each and the coxswain 6d. every week, for this duty amounting to £6.10s. per annum, for what could be done as well by one man crossing in the St Mawes steamer at 28s.2d. per annum, or by post office order at half that amount.

In July 1861, while the Coastguards were firing practice shots from the castle at a target outside the harbour, a boat manned by Mr Pascoe received a direct hit. Pascoe was severely injured and his companion had a narrow escape. In a report it was stated that: 'it is surprising that more accidents of a similar kind have not occurred by the firing into the harbour so much frequented by boats.'

Old St Mawes, with its thatched cottages and stone chimneys, c.1900.

These old cottages, built almost on the beach, became the site of the Idle Rocks hotel.

CHAPTER 3

Borough Town

The year 1562 saw St Mawes granted the privilege of becoming a Borough Town, and thus having the right to elect and send two members to Parliament. St Mawes at that time was divided into two manors, Bogullas and Lavausa. The latter, although substantially smaller than Bogullas, with its manor house and many acres of farm land, held the privileges connected with the river, including all harbour dues and fishing and anchorage rights. The dividing line between the two manors was a gutter which ran down Grove Hill and into the harbour.

The Members of Parliament were to be elected by the 'freeholders and free men of the borough', who varied in number through the years from 20 to 40 persons. A guide-book published in 1817 reported:

St Mawes is governed by a port-reeve who is complimented with the title of Mayor and sends two members to Parliament. This privilege was conferred in the fifth year of the reign of Queen Elizabeth and the right of election vested in the mayor and resident burgess who, at present, amount to about twenty. The town is of very remote origin and is supposed to have existed prior to the days of Christianity. An ancient chapel was formerly in the town, but that has been demolished and a new chapel was erected at the expense of the late Marquis of Buckingham, whose family possesses the chief influence and property of the borough. The town is principally inhabited by persons concerned in the fishery.

In 1822 the lord of the manor, the Duke of Buckingham, presented a silver gilt crowned mace to St Mawes. After it had been carried in front of the last Mayor, Edward Burtenshaw Sugden, in 1835, it was returned to the Duke. Sir Edward Sugden went on to become Lord Chancellor.

Old Court House on Marine Parade was where the Manor Courts were held.

Back in 1613 Mr Jago, who was mayor of St Mawes, was also the local customs man, a duty which he took very seriously indeed.

One morning, he observed a local man, Mr Williamson, rowing his boat back from Falmouth carrying several parcels on board. The ever-alert and, some would say, untrusting, Mr Jago rushed

The Watch House tea rooms in the 1940s. On the corner the Ship and Catle, and next to the Watchhouse, stands the old building where Joe Dotson stored his coal.

This old thatched cottage still clings to rocks on which it was built.

Local children pose for the camera, c.1900. In the background are the old cottages and Davy's bake-house, now the site of the Idle Rocks Hotel.

Old cottages and Davy's bake-house, now the site of the Idle Rocks Hotel.

This old view of St Mawes shows the old dividing wall (arrowed) halfway along the street.

The Idle Rocks Hotel, early 1950s, seen through the rigging of a trading vessel.

This view of the village in the 1950s clearly shows the old net and fish stores which were demolished in the early 1960s and replaced by a row of shops with flats.

The old net stores, seen at the extreme left, which were later used to store coal.

down to the beach and, as soon as the boat was pulled ashore, marked the parcels and the boat with a chalk-mark in the form of an arrow to show that they had been impounded by his good self.

At this, Mr Williamson removed some of his cargo, saying that it was all completely legitimate. 'Damn you!' shouted Jago. 'Deliver what you have.'

In the struggle that followed, Mr Jago gained possession of the boxes and impounded the whole cargo. Some time later, a friend of Williamson complained to the Commissioners of Customs at Falmouth and was told that the property in question had never reached the Customs House and that no one had any idea what had happened to it.

In 1537 the *Magdalen* of Truro was carrying to Brittany a number of pilgrims who were under the care of three priests. Alexander Carnanell, who was the deputy searcher at Truro, boarded the ship and was 'stricken upon the arm with a staff whereby he lost his hold and was like to perish into the salt sea.'

The ship left for St Mawes, where Alexander boarded her again, this time with two assistants.

The ship's company made their sentiments clear: 'We would not, for King nor Queen, tarry to be searched,' adding, 'If ye search here, ye shall overboard or into Brittany.'

With this they set sail and, five miles out, put Carnanell's two assistants into a small boat and cast them off.

The unfortunate Alexander was told that he would have plenty of time to 'learn to search in Brittany', while some of the crew shouted, 'Cast him

Joe Dotson delivering coal with his horse and cart, c.1940.

17

Joe Dotson delivering coal with his horse and cart.

overboard and with a rope tow him at the stern.'

When they landed at Lantregar, his captors made sure that the Bretons 'picked him quarrels, dayly shouldering and buffeting him as though he had been a Turk or a Saracen.'

It was 22 days before help arrived in the form of Nicholas Pentecost of Helford, who happened to come into the port aboard his boat, the *Anne*. On his return to Cornwall, Alexander Carnanell named some 50 persons who he held responsible for his abduction, among them the parish priests of Newlyn and St Agnes, John Michell of Truro and the captain, Richard Barrett of Truro.

St Mawes lost its rights in 1832, when the Reform Bill became law. Reading through the list of MPs, it becomes clear that they were mostly from the high-ranking families in Cornwall at that time. The Onslows, Arundells, Godolphins, Sprys and Boscawens, along with the Tredenhams, originally from Probus, provided members of Parliament from 1658 to 1710.

In 1842 the whole town was put up for sale by the lord of the manor, the Marquess of Buckingham, and was advertised as:

The whole Town of St Mawes containing about 60 dwelling houses, the Fountain Inn the St Mawes Arms, commodious fish cellars, numerous private residences and several acres of very eligible building land extending to the Castle.

CHAPTER 4

Smuggling

Smuggling was rife on the south coast of Cornwall throughout the seventeenth and eighteenth centuries, and well into the nineteenth. In an attempt to frustrate this illicit trade, the Customs Commissioners stationed teams of tidesmen and boatmen at strategic points around the coast, their job being to control regular trade and to intercept smugglers in the act of running prohibited goods. How effective these customs-house officers were is debatable, but frequent seizures were made, as the Custom House Sales advertised from time to time. The seized goods were sold, with half the proceeds going to the Crown and the other half to the seizing officers as an encouragement.

There were occasional newspaper reports of smuggling incidents and seizures. On 7 June 1792 it was reported in the *Exeter Gazette* that:

Last Friday night at Fowey a boat with 7 men belonging to the Spider cutter, went out of harbour in search of a small smuggling vessel that was expected there that night. The next morning 5 of them returned in a boat belonging to Polperro, laden with 60 casks of spirit and some tea, which they had seized a few miles to the east of the harbour. Leaving the other two in their own boat, to put the smugglers ashore at Polperro, which they did; but in their returning to Fowey a gale of wind sprung up, which drove them off shore, and they might, in all probability, have perished, had not a vessel providentially met them at sea, taken them on board, and carried them to St Mawes.

The officers were clearly more interested in seizing the goods than apprehending the smugglers, being so obliging as to take them home after the seizure.

Also in 1792 a sharp-eyed customs man, Thomas Duke, landed at St Mawes to enlist the help of the local officers. He had a strong suspicion that a quantity of smuggled spirits sunk in Gerrans Bay had been retrieved that day by the smugglers. Acting on local information they proceeded to King Harry Passage and hid in the woods. That evening they saw nine horses laden with casks and guarded by 11 men, most of them on horseback, coming along the road. The officers called for the party to halt and give up their booty. A violent struggle broke out and one of the smugglers, Joseph Tiddy, pulled out a pistol and was wrestled to the ground. As the fighting escalated, Tiddy rushed at Robert Jago and grabbed the officer's pistol, which was cut from his hand by another of the customs men. Tiddy then quickly joined the other smugglers and, arming himself with stones and shouting, 'Stones, stones, one and all we will sooner die than lose any of our goods and horses,' began throwing the stones at the officers. The customs men managed to seize seven horses and 17 casks containing 64 gallons of brandy, 32 gallons of rum and 40 gallons of Geneva. While the men were stowing the casks into the customs boat the smugglers rushed forward and managed to retrieve the horses.

Some days later Joseph Tiddy was arrested in Helston but, while being escorted from that town, he was rescued. It would be a further six years before the long arm of the law caught up with Joseph Tiddy.

At St Mawes in 1794 the customs men were Robert Jago (tide surveyor) Nicholas Sharrock, Benjamin Napton, Nicholas Cock, Samuel Bryant and Francis Symons, all boatmen of St Mawes. On 4 July, in Veryan Bay, they discovered a 'boat to which they instantly gave chase and on coming near her saw three men very busy in throwing a number of things over board which appeared to be casks.' There they discovered between 40 and 50 small barrels floating in the water. On further examination these were found to be full of brandy and Geneva. The customs men then ordered the smugglers to assist them in securing the barrels. After some hesitation they agreed, but before they had a chance to get the cargo aboard another boat with several men came alongside. One of the smugglers, Anthony Viant, boarded this boat, which was quickly rowed towards shore. The customs men gave chase and eventually caught up with the boat. On board they found Viant, a Mevagissy man, and John Williams, Bovey Williams, Samuel Mofs, Francis Hall, John Benallack and William Penrose, all from the parish of Veryan. Although the smugglers were caught, they had no intention of giving up quietly. A great deal of riotous and threatening behaviour ensued and some of the casks were opened and drunk from. Eventually, the customs men regained the illicit cargo and returned to St Mawes at midnight. We assume that the smugglers were left free to smuggle another day.

Top and above: *St Mawes Congregational Chapel.*

Φ CHAPTER 5 Φ

Church and Chapel

St Mawes has always been part of the Parish of St Just in Roseland. The rector of St Just, as early as 1381, is recorded as being licensed to celebrate in the Chapel of St Mawes, now site of Holy Well Cottage next to the Saint's well. Alongside the chapel at that time was a cemetery.

In 1505, Bishop Oldham granted a 'licence to parishioners of St Just to hear divine service in the chapel of St Maudetus before going to sea.' In the reigns of Elizabeth I and James I, the rectors seem to have discontinued services at St Mawes, and in 1621 the inhabitants petitioned Parliament for their renewal, pleading, among other reasons, the distance to St Just Church. The petition came to nothing, and in 1700 the south chancel aisle at St Just was set aside for the seating of the mayor and burgesses of St Mawes.

In the 1100s, a furious row had broken out as to who owned the Church of St Just in Roseland. The Lords of Tolverne had claimed all rights since the Norman Conquest, but in 1085 the Bishop of Exeter gave St Just and all its tithes to Plymouth Priory. As a result, for the next 50 years, St Just and Tolverne

each appointed a vicar to that parish, the two men having to share the living.

It was the custom of the local clergy, 200 years later, to have the choice of the best garment or second best beast of any of the deceased he was called on to bury. In those days of extreme poverty, this did little to endear the local vicar to his community.

The rector of St Just in 1396, Sir Thomas Raulyn, who claimed his due after the burial of one of his parishioners, 'was threatened with his life' by the distraught relatives. Taking these threats very seriously, the rector took refuge in his church.

In 1572 the rector of St Just was John Vivian, a member of that prominent Cornish family, who is recorded as leaving his living at St Just in 1576, being 'much troubled by his conscience'. Like many other rectors at that time, he was drawn to the Catholic faith. At a college set up in Rome to train these recusants, many of those attending were from Cornwall.

I note with interest that the 'chief mainstay' of the Catholic movement in Cornwall was the Arundel family, one time lords of the manors of Tolverne and St Mawes. When John Vivian had passed through

The interior of St Mawes Congregational Chapel.

Above and below: *Scenes from the United Methodist annual Sunday-school treat, 1910.*

Teachers' Group at the United Methodist annual Sunday-school treat, 1910.

The United Methodist annual Sunday-school treat, 1910.

St Just Church.

St Mawes Church.

Inside view of the Congregational Church at St Mawes.

A baby show in the grounds of St Mawes Church, c.1900.

the college, was made a priest and returned to England. Within a short time, however, he was imprisoned and in 1585, along with many other Catholic priests, was sent out of the country.

In 1807 the Marquess of Buckingham, who was lord of the manor and largely controlled the elections to Parliament, donated a site and contributed the money to build a new church at St Mawes. This was finished in 1812 but was never consecrated, owing to the opposition of the then rector of St Just, Dr Rodd. His successor, however, in 1831, asked that it might be licensed as a chapel of ease to St Just. In 1884 it was pulled down, and the present church erected on the same site.

One can hardly pick up any form of guide-book on Cornwall without seeing a picture of the Church at St Just. The very situation of the place has given rise to the legend that Christ landed there while accompanying Joseph of Arimathea, who had sailed to these shores to purchase Cornish tin. Whether this story holds any water or not, I shall leave to the judgement of the individual, but few would dispute the beauty and serenity of the place, with its abundance of flowering shrubs and its backdrop of St Just creek.

We cannot say for sure when Methodism arrived on the Roseland, but a chapel was built in St Mawes in 1803. When this chapel was registered in 1807, the trustees were named as Jos Hooker, John Vivian, John Kemp, John Hooker and Faithful Blitchford. Nothing more is known about the chapel or its site.

A lease signed on 25 December 1816 by James Buller and Thomas Hooker states that the latter; 'intends to erect and build a large and convenient Methodist chapel and to lay out in building the same the sum of £400, at least'. By 2 June 1817 the chapel was completed and the trustees are named as John Snell, yeoman, and Thomas Olive, cooper, both of Gerrans; John Luke, miller, of St Anthony; Philip Varco, mason; Jos Hooker, cordwainer; Samual Hooker, smith; John Varco, tailor; William Watts, cordwainer; Robert Nuget, schoolmaster; James Swords, hatter and Theodosius Harris Pasco, boat-builder (all of St Mawes). The chapel cost £600 to build and on its opening, only £100 had been raised.

In 1826 St Mawes became the head of the newly formed Roseland Methodist circuit. At a quarterly meeting held at Treworlas on 26 December 1845 it was agreed that: 'the trustees of the Wesleyan chapel at St Mawes be requested to build a house on the trust property adjoining that Chapel, for the use of the Minister stationed in the St Mawes circuit.'

In 1862 a day-school was added at a cost of £200. This was the first purpose-built school in St Mawes and opened in the September of that year, with eight children in class two and 11 in class three, some of them as young as four years old. Within 12 months there were over 100 pupils, ranging in age from two to 15 years, each child being charged 2d. per week for the privilege of attending. This school continued until 1894, when the present school was built.

St Mawes was also the head of the Bible Christian

<u>Senior Division (for Candidates over 18).</u>

Congregational Union of England & Wales
YOUNG PEOPLE'S DEPARTMENT.

Examination : "OLIVER CROMWELL."
FRIDAY, DECEMBER 5th, 1924.

Examiner : Rev. W. Melville Harris, M.A.

Text Book : "Oliver Cromwell: England's Uncrowned King."
By Rev. Albert Peel, M.A., Litt.D.

EIGHT questions *only* to be answered, which should include 1 and 3. 24 marks possible for each answer, with an additional 4 marks each for Nos. 1 and 3. Maximum marks—**200**. Time allowed—Two and half hours.

1. Summarise the verdict of his contemporaries on Cromwell's character, and estimate it from your own standpoint.

2. Give a brief account of Cromwell's life up to his marriage, indicating how early training fitted him for his later career.

3. Laud affirmed that there could be "no unity without uniformity." Discuss this statement in the light of subsequent events.

4. Relate in brief the events in the Government of Strafford and Laud as they influenced later history.

5. State the tasks that confronted the Long Parliament on its assembling and Cromwell's attitude to them.

6. Cromwell said the Civil War was undertaken for "the maintenance of our civil liberties as men, and our religious liberties as Christians." How far were these aims subsequently realised ?

7. Consider if Milton was right when he said : "New presbyter is but old priest writ large." Point out the difference between Presbyterianism and Independency.

8. Discuss the triangular fight of Crown, Parliament, and Army after the Battle of Naseby.

9. Relate the circumstances that led up to the "cruel necessity" of the execution of Charles I.

10. Describe the effect of Cromwell's foreign policy when he was Protector.

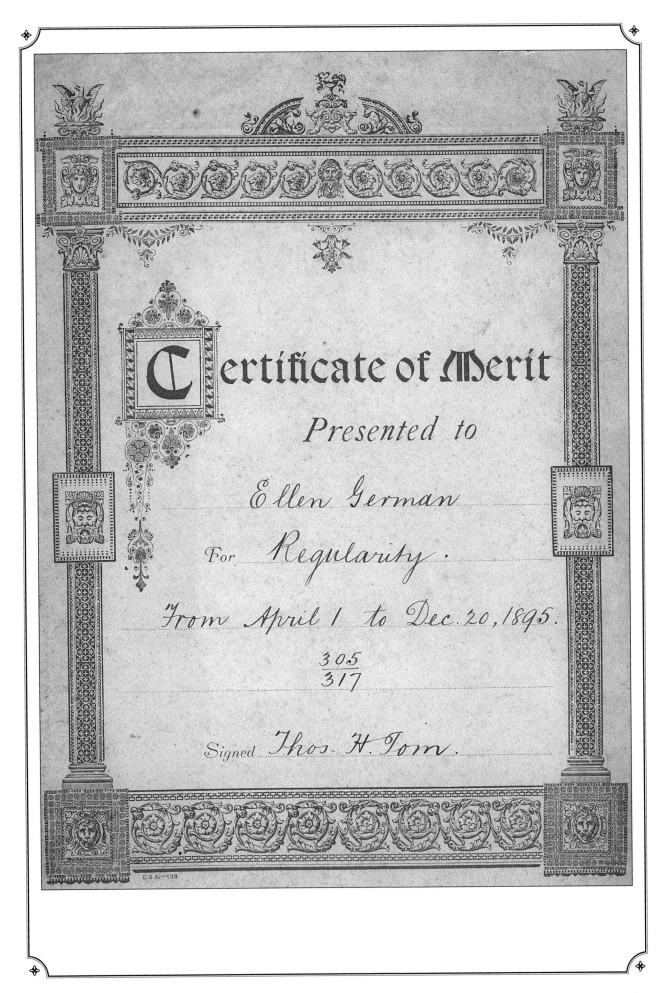

Certificate of Merit

Presented to

Ellen German

For Regularity.

From April 1 to Dec. 20, 1895.

$$\frac{305}{317}$$

Signed Thos. H. Tom.

E.S.A.—139.

Children at the United Methodist annual Sunday-school treat, 1910.

circuit in the Roseland. It had been separated from the Mevagissey circuit in 1866, when its meeting-house occupied the site of Holy Well Cottage. For some reason, probably because larger premises were needed, a new chapel was built in 1874.

On Christmas Day the following year, the new chapel was opened by the Revd F.W. Bourne, regarded as the greatest figure in the Bible Christian movement. This must have been a very successful day, almost half of the total cost of £542 being raised. A Sunday-school room, part of the original premises, was improved in 1896 at a cost of £91, and in 1920 the freehold was purchased at a cost of £1,250. This chapel now serves as the Roman Catholic church.

St Mawes Congregational Church was opened on Good Friday 1809. The first minister was Revd Bevan, who had previously trained for ministry in the Church of England. At its 100th anniversary service in 1909 there was an 'over-flowing audience'. In the early 1920s, under the ministry of Revd T.H. Emanuel, who had come to St Mawes from South Wales, the attendances were once more greatly increased.

The following year, it was reported, there were 'unmistakeable signs of social and spiritual recovery', and attendances for the 'morning service nigh on doubled'. The attendance figures far outstripped those of Tregony and Portscatho.

Among a long list of ministers, James Gant stands out as an asset to the village. Born in 1803 in Mawnan Smith, Gant, orphaned at an early age, was made a free scholar of St Mawes School, where his father had at one time been the master. At the age of 16 he opened his own schoolroom under the patronage of the Duke of Buckingham, who was a great patron of the borough. In 1829 he was led, through unknown circumstances, to become the minister of the Independent Church in St Mawes. It is said that he was fluent in Hebrew, Greek, Latin, German and French, and that he often used these languages in his services. To the local people, whether of his own denomination or not, he always seems to have been available:

All in the Town found him in their difficulties and there a ready helper and wise counsellor. To the fishermen of St Mawes he was a friend and benefactor. He fought for them many a hard battle when their plights and inter-ests were imperilled, sparing neither thought, nor time nor money in order to preserve them and long will his name continue to be a household word in their homes.

In 1902 a scandal emerged which not only rocked the Congregational Church at St Mawes, but which must have had reverberations around the whole area. A special church meeting was called, attended by 26 members, to discuss allegations of sexual misconduct between the wife of a church official and a member of the congregation. The lady in question was expelled from the church and her lover was banned from attending any further church services.

CHAPTER 6

Old Families

St Mawes was made up of a nucleus of old families and, happily, some of them are still very much in evidence today. The names Green, Tiddy, German, Hancock, Dotson, Collins, Clode, Ferris and Sawle, along with many others, have all played their part in the history of the village.

The Wesleyan circuit recorded 16 Green family baptisms between 1841 and 1898. The family are easily traced back to 1733, when William Green was born. He went on to marry Rebecca Wakum in 1754 and it would seem that most of the branches of the Green family stem from their union.

The Dotsons seem to have sailed over from Mylor in the early 1800s and were soon occupying themselves in the fishing, innkeeping and piloting trades.

In the Protestation Returns of 1641, Ambrose Jenkin, Nicholas Mitchell, Alexander Harris, Thomas Lelean and Inigo Vincent are all mentioned, giving their families a longevity of over 300 years. Luckily, a good number of old photos of local people have survived, tucked away in boxes and albums.

When the young men and women of St Mawes left school they were expected to go straight into employment and, with so many trades carried on within the perimeters of the village, this was not too difficult. Luckily, because indentures had to be drawn up on such occasions, we are left with a record of who worked for whom. In 1878 Charles Hooper Greet was apprenticed to James Dash, a Trinity pilot. The following July, George Green was apprenticed to Richard Green for a period of six years. George was also to be schooled as a pilot. In 1874 William James Pascoe was bound to local mason William Pascoe. William James would go on to become a well-known builder in and around St Mawes, building several properties in the village.

Mr and Mrs Hide, c.1880.

Coastguard Thomas Dillon, c.1880, who was stationed at St Mawes.

Ambrose and Elizabeth Green, a portrait c.1800.

Cyril Green, c.1900.

Granny Collins, c.1900.

Grandfather Collins, early 1900s.

Joe Vincent, 1880.

Joe Collins, 1880.

Granny Collins, c.1900.

Katie Edwards, c.1900.

John Green, c.1900.

Richard German, c.1900.

Roland Vincent, c.1900.

Katie Pasco, c.1900.

James Collins, c.1900.

Nat Collins, c.1900.

Jack Collett, c.1900.

Addie Collett, c.1900.

Edward Inkerman Green, c.1900.   *Tom Sawle, c.1900.*

In Loving Memory

OF

ROBERT,

The dearly beloved husband of M. L. Harris, of Gibraltar House,
St. Mawes,

Who entered into rest, June 24th, 1898,

AGED 37 YEARS.

" Thanks be to God which giveth us the victory,
through our Lord Jesus Christ."

William German and James Collins, c.1900.

Henry and Mary Andain, who were married in 1834.

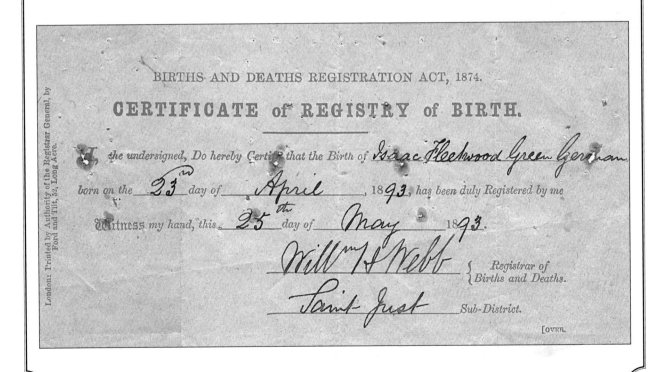

Rhoda Thomas, c.1900.

Hubert Andain, c.1910.

Mary Andain, c.1900.

Granny and Grandfather Sawle, c.1900.

Above: *Beatrice Sheba Sawle, Jack Watts and Emma Adeline Collins, 1900s.*

Emma Collins, c.1900.

Fleetwood German, 1905.

Amelia Thomas (née Peters), 1930. She came to St Mawes from Falmouth as an infant and was brought up by the Peters family.

The Collins family c.1900 with, from left to right: Joseph Collins, Granny Collins, Grandfather Collins, Addie Collins.

Collins family wedding, 1912.

Winifred Dash, 1920.

Sam and Joe Dotson, c.1920.

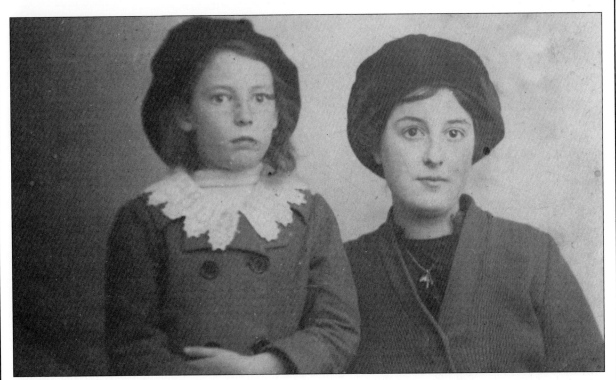

Muriel Dotson, pictured in 1921 with her aunt Annie German (right), who married the well-known Cornish athlete Jim Pollard, from Gerrans.

Some old and not so old salts relaxing on the quay in the 1920s.

A view of the village in 1928.

Tommy Green, c.1930.

Emma German, c.1930.

Grandfather Collins aboard his boat, c.1930.

Sam Dotson enjoying the river, c.1950.

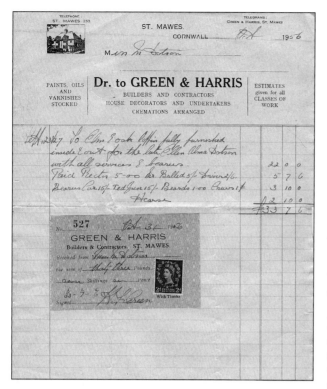

The following year Edward Dotson was indentured to Samuel Francis Lowry.

Occasionally these indentures were transferred or cancelled. Sharrock Vincent, who had been apprenticed to Henry Vincent in 1871, had his indenture cancelled in 1877 because he had 'gone to sea' in 1881. Sharrock's father, also Sharrock, was a baker living and working in St Mawes.

In a slightly different surviving indenture, dated 1745, between the Rt Hon. Hugh Lord, Viscount Falmouth, and William Lowry, fisherman, of the parish of St Just in Roseland, the indenture reads:

Viscount Falmouth for the sum of twelve pounds and twelve shillings of good lawful money of Great Briton grants a Dwelling house, Court ledges and Backsides with all the appurtenances situated and lying and being in Bohilla in St Just.

The house in question had been the abode of Michael Jenkins, who had recently died. The lease stated that Michael was aged 'about twenty nine years and his son William aged about seven years'. With a rent fixed at 6s.8d., the lease would run for 99 years or the rest of their lives. This house was situated in St Austell Row.

The 1841 *Kelly's Directory* noted that James Peters was running the Post Office. Letters were scheduled to arrive at noon, with the afternoon post leaving at 1.30p.m. The local surgeon at the time was Lawrence Boyne, Mr Nicholas Teddy being the master at the school.

One thing that St Mawes was not short of was shoemakers, with William Webber, Henry Vincent, James Toy, John Spry, John Jordan and Robert Jenkin

all plying their trade in the town. William Peters and Robert Smith were both building boats and the associated trade of carpenter\joiner was well represented by Richard Bellman, Solomon Borlase, Rice Lowry and William Stanton.

Richard Chenoweth and Philip Varco were both earning a living as masons, while small shops were run by Jane Vincent, Ann Rickard, James Peters, Elizabeth Jones, Grace Jago and Catherine and Mary Blake. These little shops, often trading from a room in a cottage, catered for everyday needs, selling all manner of groceries.

There was also a tailor in the town. John (Saul) Sawle was busy making and repairing clothes, while William Blake was busy working as a rope maker.

Just a look at this list gives a good picture of the town at that time, with almost all everyday needs catered for, from new ropes to tea and shoes.

The following year traders throughout the Roseland were visited by the Inspector of Weights and Measures. The gentleman concerned carried out spot checks throughout the area, mainly on dealers in tea, tobacco and snuff, and 45 traders, including nearly all the retailers of St Mawes, were found guilty of using 'unjust weights' when they were brought before the magistrates at Ruan High Lanes. A report on the case in the *West Briton* revealed that:

... they were amerced in small fines, and their inaccurate beams and scales (comprising nearly a cart load of such rubbish as was never seen in the Court before) were condemned to be, demolished.

The plans for a railway linking the Roseland with the district of St Austell thankfully never materialised, otherwise our peninsula would not have retained the charm and rural splendour that we treasure so much today. The idea first came to light in 1832, with the vision of providing:

Cheap conveyance of lime, manure etc, to improve agriculture in the Roseland and to reclaim the moors along the Fal, to supply iron, coal and groceries cheaply to the Roseland, Tregony and Grampound and to take mine products from the Roche area to be shipped from Falmouth harbour. This would lessen the need for horses to carry and haul goods and so enable the farmer to increase his bullocks, sheep and livestock and extend the growth of corn and flax.

The main supporter of this scheme was John Penhallow Peters of Philleigh. After ten years of negotiations, the plan was dropped, only to raise its ugly head again in 1912:

The new St Just railway project is amongst the schemes to be submitted to Parliament during the forthcoming session. A bill will be promoted to incorporate a company with power to construct a railway,

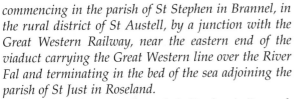

Joe Dotson outside Grove Cottage.

Tommy Clode enjoying a pint in the 1960s.

commencing in the parish of St Stephen in Brannel, in the rural district of St Austell, by a junction with the Great Western Railway, near the eastern end of the viaduct carrying the Great Western line over the River Fal and terminating in the bed of the sea adjoining the parish of St Just in Roseland.

The railway is to pass through St Stephen in Brannel, Creed and Grampound Road, in the district of St Austell, and Probus, Cuby, Tregony, Cornelly, Lamorran, Ruan Lanihorne, Philleigh, St Just in Roseland and Veryan. It was also proposed to construct a wharf or quay wholly in the parish of St Just.

The following week the same reporter wrote:

Considerable disappointment is expressed in the village of Gerrans that the proposed Roseland railway will not run nearer Gerrans than White Lanes (two and a half miles away). It is understood from a reliable source that the needs of Gerrans and Portscatho were considered by the promoters of the project, but it was ultimately decided not to embody the construction of a branch line in the Bill, now before Parliament, in the event of the line being constructed. However, the company will favourably consider proposals for arranging for a branch line if the suggestions are backed up by the inhabitants as being beneficial to the locality. There can be no doubt as to the advantages that would accrue to

the village, particularly in the summer time on account of its present inaccessibility to visitors.

Fortunately the whole project was dropped in 1913 due to lack of financial support.

In days gone by, the collection of income tax seems to have been a rather hit-and-miss affair. The tax collector went from village to village on foot, and in 1843 it was reported by one hard-pressed officer that, although he had walked 104 miles in six days, out of £200 owed, he had collected only 11s.6d.

The St Mawes Harbour Company was formed in 1854. Although there had been a pier here since 1536, it was in a poor state of repair, and the new company were granted an Act of Parliament to build a new pier and to dredge the harbour to enable larger vessels to berth there.

The new pier, destroyed in a ferocious storm in 1872, was rebuilt the following year. The following year the tragic deaths of two Italian seamen occurred.

On Monday, two Italian seamen belonging to a vessel in Falmouth Roads, went to the shore near the ship, to fill up water casks. They picked and ate some hemlock, mistaking it for an edible herb, and shortly after, they both died from the poison. The seamen were named Antonia Bonich, aged 24 and Giovanni Rossi, aged 27 and they belonged to the Austrian brig Guistop.'

Pat Schichtar and her mother, Esmie Clode, 1981.

Marina Penhaligon (née Clode) in 1988, serving up a cream tea.

… two sailors went to St Just creek, where they filled their casks with water for the ship, and then Rossi went into the fields for turnips and Bonich for herbs. The tide being out and the boat unable to leave the beach, they

and another sailor went to get oysters. On returning, Rossi fell down and began to howl with pain and after about ten minutes, Bonich fell down in the same way.'

Neither could speak. Foam came from their mouths and they perspired a lot. In about a quarter of an hour they seemed quite insensible. A boy sailor in the boat said he saw both the deceased eat some of the herbs produced; he also ate a little but felt nothing.

In July 1862 a young local lad had a narrow escape:

On Monday evening, a little son of Mr Dotson, of St Mawes, accidentally fell over the Quay at high water. Exertions were immediately used to save him by getting a boat to the spot as quickly as possible. Before that could be accomplished, however, the little fellow was rescued by Mr R. Rawling, of HMS Russell, who gallantly plunged into the water after him and succeeded in bringing him safely to the quay steps.

As picturesque as thatched cottages are, there is always the threat of fires spreading, like the one in 1868, when four cottages were lost.

Four cottages were burnt at St Mawes yesterday. At about eight o'clock in the morning, they were discovered to be on fire and in a short time they were completely gutted. The fire is supposed to have originated from a spark from a chimney igniting the dry thatch. The poor people inhabiting the houses were successful in saving nearly the whole of the furniture.

St Mawes

Views in and around St Mawes in the early decades of the twentieth century.

St Mawes

Later postcard views of St Mawes.

✦ CHAPTER 7 ✦

For Those in Peril

A great number of ships have come to grief on the Cornish coast throughout the years, St Mawes having had its fair share. This is not too surprising considering the vast amount of trade that the harbour of Falmouth has attracted through the centuries. It was not unusual to see 200–300 ships at anchor in the bay throughout the nineteenth century. The most important moment in the history of the port of Falmouth and the surrounding area, however, was the introduction of the packet service in 1688. Many of the packet boats were built in or near Falmouth and this, coupled with refitting and the ever-demanding market for provisions, went a long way to establishing Falmouth as a major port.

Captain William Rogers, born at Falmouth on 29 September 1773, married Susan, daughter of Captain John Harris of St Mawes. In 1807 Rogers was made master of the packet boat *Windsor Castle*, trading from Falmouth to Barbados with a complement of 28 men. On 1 October 1807, on her outward journey, she was pursued by a privateer schooner under full sail. As there seemed little chance of outrunning the schooner, Captain Rogers decided to stand and fight.

By noon, the privateer was within gunshot. She hoisted French colours and opened fire, which the packet boat immediately returned. The privateer, *Le Jeune Richard*, invited Rogers to 'strike his colours'. When he refused, grappling irons were thrown and the pirates attempted to board the packet.

The crew of the *Windsor Castle*, however, were ready with their pikes and ten of the Frenchmen were killed. The privateers tried to cut away their grappling irons but could not get clear.

At about 3p.m. a second boarding was attempted by the French, but Rogers and his crew were ready and, with guns blazing, the packet men succeeded in driving their pursuers back and captured the French ship. Though the crew of the *Windsor Castle* lost three men, with two others severely wounded, French casualties were much heavier, with 21 dead and 33 wounded.

The 38 remaining pirates were put in irons and the *Windsor Castle*, with only 15 able-bodied crew, made for Barbados.

For his courageous conduct, Rogers received the thanks of the Postmaster General, 100 guineas and his promotion to captain. He was also given the freedom of the City of London.

An amusing tale concerning Captain Rogers, which has come to light while researching this book, reads as follows:

In London, a gentleman named Dixon, unacquainted with Rogers, sought and obtained his friendship and then commissioned Samuel Drummon to make a picture of the action in which the hero's full-length portrait should appear. Whilst the painting was in progress, Rogers ran up against a man in the street so closely resembling the officer he had shot, that he caught him by the button and begged him to let the distinguished artist paint his portrait. The gentleman was not a little surprised, but when Rogers informed him who he was and why he desired to have him painted, he readily consented. He was conducted to the studio and there, stood as portrait model for the French swordsman by whom Rogers had been so nearly cut down.

On 5 December 1830 it was reported that the sailing brig *Bon Pere*, en route from Guadeloupe to Le Havre with a cargo of sugar, had been wrecked on Towan beach. The wreck of the almost new vessel produced a local hero, William James of St Mawes.

On Monday afternoon a brig was seen off Portscatho, attempting to weather the Zone point to reach Falmouth, but it was evident she was drifting rapidly towards the shore. The Coastguard under Captain Ray, were promptly mustered, and a large body of people were soon on the cliff to render assistance. About 5p.m. the brig struck on the sand on Towan Beach, the tide then rising and a tremendous surf breaking over her, and she remained in this situation about half an hour. A large fire was built on the beach to afford light to the crew, who appeared much distressed, and were loudly crying for help. The tide was rising, and Lieutenant William James RN of St Mawes stripped himself, and boldly plunging through the surf, got under the bow of the brig and brought on shore a rope, by which means the whole of the crew, ten in number, got safely on the land.

The recently built vessel was driven so high up the beach that it was impossible to get her off, but her cargo of sugar was saved.

A local newspaper reported that 'the exertions of the people to save and secure the vessel and cargo did them the highest honour.'

Lieutenant James was awarded a gold medal and four other men who had helped also received monetary awards.

In October 1859 the Swedish timber brig *Oscar* drove ashore at St Mawes in a severe storm. She was unharmed and was refloated when the storm had subsided.

In the winter of 1865, when the Barbados registered ship *Edith* was wrecked under St Mawes Castle, her fittings and stores were taken off and auctioned at Falmouth. The rest of the ship was sold, piece by piece, where she lay.

It was most unusual at the time to read a report such as this, printed in 1890:

On Sunday, Falmouth Harbour presented an unusual appearance. On the whole of the magnificent roadstead, extending from St Anthony's lighthouse to Mylor Pool, not a single vessel, with the exception of HMS Ganges was at anchor. Such a sight has not been witnessed at Falmouth for many years, although, unfortunately, there have however been times when only a very small number of vessels have been at anchor in the roadstead.

Just a few years earlier it was not uncommon to see 200–300 ships lying at anchor in Carrick Roads and in the channel leading up to Penryn, all of which brought a good deal of business to St Mawes, as well as to Mylor and Flushing.

Wreck at St Mawes, 1890

About 1.30 on Thursday morning, W. Hancock, coastguard, observed a vessel pointing straight towards the Castle Point. He fired six revolver shots to warn the crew of their danger and, as no notice seemed to be taken, he burnt a red light. This also had no effect, the vessel coining with a great crash onto the rocks.

The Chief Officer was at once informed and he proceeded to the Post office and roused the Postmaster (Mr. G.R. Cole) who telegraphed to Falmouth for the lifeboat. The coastguards then pulled to the distressed vessel, but the captain refused to leave her. The banging of a coastguard mortar between two and three o'clock in the morning warned Falmouth of something being wrong afloat. It was dreadful weather, dark and with rain falling in torrents.

A French ketch, the Louise Ernest, belonging to St Halo, had come to grief. Laden with china clay from Par, she left Falmouth on Wednesday for Nantes. Off the Lizard the seas were so heavy that the master deemed it prudent to turn back. The little ship was put about and made for Falmouth. She fetched the mouth of the harbour safely and passed in under the St Anthony lights. But instead of keeping along the roadstead, the Captain evidently missed his way in the darkness, became embayed, with the result that his ship was carried upon the rocky shore immediately beneath St Mawes Castle. The lifeboat was soon out, and took off the five occupants, four men and a boy, who were conveyed to Falmouth and received into the Royal Cornwall Sailors' Home between four and five o'clock in the morning. There they were made comfortable around the fire, and provided with breakfast before again setting out for the scene of the wreck, to see what, if anything could be done to save their ship.

At daylight the ketch as seen from a distance appeared to be held firmly by a tongue of rock, running from the mainland into the sea. The chance of getting her off was considered to be very small.

This was the first occasion that the lifeboat crew had been called into active service since their reorganisation and Mr E.T. Oliver, the local Hon. Secretary, has had the satisfaction of informing the Lifeboat institution that the new arrangements worked expeditiously and smoothly.

A later examination of the ship led those concerned to practically abandon any hope of the hull being of further service. The rocks had torn the bottom badly and water has destroyed the cargo. The crew had been able to recover their personal property but there were three dogs on board. Under new regulations these could not be landed until authority was received from the Board of Agriculture.

On 22 January 1910, the *Indefatigable*, having been weather-bound at Falmouth for a week, was towed from the harbour by the tug *Challenge*. She was bound for Cardiff, but, off Lands End, the seas were so rough that they both returned and anchored in Carrick Roads. Some time in the night the *Indefatigable* dragged her anchors and drifted across the bay, coming ashore under St Mawes Castle, and was high and dry at low water. She was pulled off by the tugs *Dragon*, *Marian* and *Briton* and towed into Falmouth, where she was dry docked. Once there, however, it was found that the repair bill would have been such that she was sold for scrap.

On 10 July 1940, in a German bombing raid on Falmouth harbour, three ships were set afire – the steamer *Marie Chandris*, the tanker *British Chancellor* and the Greek tanker *Tuscalusa*. The *Marie Chandris*, loaded with raw cotton, was soon ablaze. She was towed to a small bay near St Mawes and sunk by gunfire. Later she was patched up, refloated and beached at Place, where some of her cargo was salvaged and she was cut up for scrap. The *Tuscalusa* was towed to St Just and sunk. Here, the superstructure was cut away and was towed in sections to Freeman's Yard in Penryn.

In 1949 the *Northern Lights* came ashore in strong winds on Tavern beach. 'She came in hard, right up under the sea wall. They did manage to get her off with jacks and slid her back down the beach on planks.'

Spuds Twice a Day and Marmalade Once a Week

The young men of St Mawes have often looked to the sea for their living, some of them shipping off to distance ports on the packet ships or cargo barques.

In 1880, Edward Dotson a member of that well-

Edward Dotson.

known St Mawes family, left for London. Edward had seemed destined to follow in his father's footsteps as a longshoreman, but by the late 1870s pilotage was in decline at Falmouth, with a corresponding reduction in the demand for boatmen. Bigger ships meant fewer ships, and the great swing to steamers was eroding Falmouth's standing as an 'orders port'. With the decline in shipping traffic there were more pilots and pilot-cutters than the trade could stand, and in 1884 the port pilot service was forced to reorganise as a co-operative and reduce its numbers. The prospects were not good for casual employment.

Under these circumstances Edward and Francis Denton, possibly childhood companions, decided to try their luck 'deep sea'. Both had previously served on the *Pollu* of St Mawes. By the winter of 1879–80 they had made their way to London and signed on as able seamen aboard the iron barque *Himalaya*, then under the command of Captain Culbert. Registered at Southampton, the *Himalaya* was far from a new vessel, having been completed in 1863. She had already completed several voyages between England and New Zealand and was one of the first ships to pioneer refrigeration, bringing home frozen lamb.

On 28 January 1880 our two St Mawes lads were paid one month's wages in advance, amounting to £2.10s. each, and we can only assume that they had a good run ashore before leaving.

With pre-voyage formalities quickly completed, the barque cleared customs on the following day. A week later she sailed from Gravesend, passing Deal the next day on her run down the channel at the outset of her 11,000 mile plus voyage.

Some 100 days later, on 17 May 1880, the *Himalaya* berthed at Wellington, where Edward and Frank deserted after one week in port, along with seven other hands and one of the apprentices, thereby forfeiting any wages then due. Edward did not tell those at home that he had deserted, but in his second letter home to his father gave his reason for leaving her as 'there was nothing but a lot of Welshmen on board', which could not have been further from the truth. There was not a single Welshman in the crew, though there were ten foreign seamen – mostly Scandinavians. It is possible that he mistook their foreign tongue for Welsh, but very likely it was just a prejudicial excuse, which he must have expected his father to accept with approval.

Leaving the *Himalaya* in Wellington on 6 June, Edward and Frank went up-country to try their luck in the bush. This proved no more financially rewarding than seafaring, and they found it very tough going, with little to show for their efforts. The best part of three months later, after having been unable to earn more than their keep, they returned to Wellington, where they were both happy to find berths on board the Glasgow barque *Rodell Bay*, under the command of Captain Lindsay, bound for San Francisco in ballast to ship a cargo of wheat for home. It turned out to be a fateful decision.

The *Rodell Bay* was a much newer vessel than the *Himalaya*, having been completed by Dobie & Co. of Glasgow in January 1877, though both vessels were much the same size. As can be seen from her articles of agreement, the *Rodell* was also carrying passengers: 'Any member of the crew interfering in any way with the passengers will forfeit one month's pay, or be handed over to the authorities on the ship's arrival.'

Just two days before she sailed, Edward wrote the first of his two surviving letters home:

Wellington
15 Sep 1880

Dear, Father Mother Brothers and Sisters,
Just a few lines to let you know how we are getting on trusting it will find you all in good health as I am happy to let you know it leaves us both at present. We have been expecting a letter by each mail but I am afraid we shall be gone before the next mail comes in. We shall be leaving New Zealand about the 18th. We haven't had no letters from home since we left Himalaya. We have been working in the bush for about three months and thought it most time that we cleared out as it was hard

work and very little pay. We came in town and shipped aboard a large iron barque, Rodell Bay, of Glasgow. We are bound for San Francisco and then to Falmouth for orders. We shall be about 7 or 8 months. It is very bad times in New Zealand. At present, there isn't much work for any of the working class. They are sending out to many immigrants. There are plenty of chaps out here who just work for their tucker, as we had to do for a little while dear father. I have not much more to say about myself.

We have employed ourselves pretty well and plenty of hard work. I don't think we shall want any new suits when we get home as I don't think we are grown much more than when we left.

Dear Father, Mr John Harvey sends home his kindest and best regards to you hoping it will find you well. Dear Father I must conclude for the time hoping to write you a longer one from Frisco. Give my kindest and best love to Mother, John, Billy, Samuel, Joe and Agnes. I suppose she is a fine woman by this time. Grandmother Aunt Odgers, Uncle John, Aunt Emma, John, Arthur, Janey and all her family, Aunt Hilde and Uncle Addie, Mr & Mrs Pearce, Uncle Joseph and his wife, Mahala, Mrs Dillon to Joe and No 8 (pilot boat) Mr Loury, Jemmie, Joe, Ned, Jack Webb and all inquiring friends and accept the same from your loving son Edward Dotson. Tell John to give my best regards to all his chummies. Good Bye God Bless.

The next letter Edward's father received was written from San Francisco in November:

Barque Rodell Bay
San Francisco
November 21\81

Dear, Father and Mother, Brothers and Sisters.
I write you a few lines after a long absence, trusting it will meet you all in good health as I am happy to let you know it leaves me at present. I should have written you as soon as we arrived. I only waited to see if I should get a letter from you. I haven't had neither one yet. We arrived in Frisco on the 9th after a passage of 55 days with fine weather all the way.

We have got all our Ballast out and took in part of our cargo for stiffening, then we were towed about 40 miles

up the Sacramento river for the rest of the cargo. I expect we shall be sailing in about a week's time. We are going for orders, Falmouth or Queenstown.

Dear Father, I suppose you have been thinking a great deal about me. I dare say I should have been home about this time if I stopped by the Himalaya, but with a lot of Welsh on board, we should be only three Englishmen there if we stopped. The Rodell is a large Barque, nearly two thousand tons. We are all English chaps on board and we have great good times and very good grub. We get spuds twice a day and a tin of marmalade every week.

There are fine lot of ships here loading for home and the best part for orders. I suppose piloting is a little better now, than when we left. I dare say Joe is still in the boat. I should like to have had a parcel from home and to read a little of the news. I suppose Addie is still at the school and Agnes, I shouldn't know her by the time I get back. I don't think I have grown much myself. I suppose not for the want of posh grub.

Give my kindest and best love to Mother and John, Billy, Samuel, Joseph and Agnes, Grandmother, Aunt Ada, Uncle Joseph, Mr and Mrs Pearce, Mr Lowery, E Nicholls and J Hodge.

Your Loving Son, Edward Dotson

When Edward noted that 'there are a fine lot a ships here loading for home and best part is going for orders', he was not overstating the fact. During the 20 days that they were in port, some 32 other vessels came in to load wheat for England. Although when he wrote he thought they were going for orders to Falmouth, they actually cleared for Queenstown on 29 November.

Clearing for Queenstown on that date, the *Rodell Bay*, commanded by Captain Lindsley, sailed on 3 December never to be heard of again. The average passage time that year from San Francisco to Queenstown or Falmouth was about 130 days, or about four and half months at sea. As Edward anticipated, April should have seen her in home waters, but it did not.

Edward never saw St Mawes again. A memorial stone in St Just churchyard records: 'Edward Dotson, who died at sea 1881, aged 24 years'.

CHAPTER 8

Fishing

'Pilchards are food, money and light, all in one night.'

Before the tourist trade had ever been thought of, fishing was the life blood of St Mawes, with the majority of families in the village, in one way or another, being involved in it. Cornish pilchards were, shipped overseas in their hundreds of thousands throughout the eighteenth and nineteenth centuries. The pilchards were caught in seine nets and brought to the fish cellars, which were open-fronted sheds. Here they were packed into barrels with layers of salt and weighed down with heavy stones to squeeze out the oil.

At that time there were a large number of these cellars in St Mawes – a map drawn up in 1772 marks fish cellars all along the village waterfront. On the site of the Ship & Castle, fish cellars, salt cellars and fish sheds are recorded. On the same map Nos. 12 and 13 Marine Parade were home to a cooper producing barrels for the pilchard trade. Next door, at No. 14, a carpenter's shop is shown, and a school-room, while another cooper's shop can be found at

No. 15. By 1840 fish cellars had been built to the north of Tredenham Road and at Sea View Crescent. The oil extracted from the fish was highly prized and went to light lamps not only in local cottages but also on the streets of London.

With such a busy fishing industry, rope makers were employed within the village. There were rope works, or rope walks, as they were known, at Newton Farm and also at what is still known as the Rope Walk.

The time of the greatest activity was the late summer, when huge shoals of mackerel and pilchards appeared off the south-west coast. For a few frantic weeks the people of St Mawes, as did their counterparts in other fishing villages up and down the coast, worked from morning until night, salting down their catch.

In 1788 the Revd S. Shaw wrote:

A very fine oil is produced from these fish, which they

The Onward pilchard seine, 1906.

pile up in great heaps as long and broad as the house made for the purpose will permit, and breast high. Then, with proper boards, weights, etc, they press the oil out into a gutter, which communicates with a vessel fixed in the ground at one end of the house.

This oil was known as train oil.

A sale was held at the St Mawes Arms on 19 October 1801:

The Adventure stop and tuck seines, made wholly with Bridport Twine, together with the boats and all other Materials thereunto belonging; the whole of which have been made eight, and have been at sea only six years, and are in remarkable good order, now lying at Polvarth, near St Mawes.

The pilchard men worked on a share basis, each member of the crew being expected to put money into the venture and then suffer the losses and take a percentage of the profits when they accrued. At a sale held in St Mawes in 1813 one of the seine boats changed hands. Anyone wishing to buy in would have had to bid for part of the lots on offer. They consisted of 6,000 barrel makers' rods, 2,500 pilchard casks, 340 empty barrels, 40 oil casks and 2,000 barrel staves, as well as a large quantity of baskets and lengths of rope.

The *Royal Cornwall Gazette* reported that 1812 had been a good season for pilchards and that they were selling for 3d. a hundred – 'Plentiful fish, with a good crop of potatoes, has greatly relieved the state of the poor.'

This low price, however, did little to help the hard-pressed fishermen of the Roseland.

Offered for tender (May 1816) by William Blake & Co. of St Mawes, an eighth share in the Hope seine at the Lizard, consisting of 2 stop seines one tuck seine and two seine boats.

When the Active seine was offered for sale at Polvarth in 1823, it was stated that: 'As a situation for the Pilchard Fishery, St Mawes is justly considered the Best in Cornwall.'

In 1826 there were ten seine boats operating out of St Mawes, which gave employment to 155 men. In that year, the Friendship seine, consisting of two stop and one tuck seines, two seine boats and two lurkers, was offered for sale. The nets were unfit and were cut up and sold in small lots to local gardeners. Several other seines were offered for sale in the next few years and the very number of them confirms that St Mawes was indeed a hive of activity in the hey-day of the pilchard.

As has already been stated, the Active seine was offered for sale in 1823, followed by the Unity and the Lord Exmouth in 1825. Other seines offered for sale included the Trust, the Prosperous and the

Exmouth in 1826, the Friendship in 1827, the St Mawes in 1828, the Prosperous in 1829, the Olive Branch, which was lying at Blake's Cellars, new in 1816, the Endeavour, lying at Blake's Cellars, repaired in 1827 with new netting 'which has not been wetted since', and in 1832 the Adventure seine was put up for sale at Percuil.

In 1826, William Blake & Co. went out of business and their premises – two cellars, a cooperage and a bark shed – were put up for sale, along with shares in the Trusty, the Olive Branch and the Diamond seines.

On 27 August 1832 the Cumberland seine was shot off St Mawes Castle and 500 hogsheads were landed. The following year, however, pilchards were few and far between, and it was reported that many of the families in St Mawes and Portloe were near starvation. This was partly due to the fact that the drift boats were able to intercept the shoals of pilchards out at sea, so robbing the inshore seiners of their bounty.

A report published in 1869 stated that the St Mawes seiners could fish four miles along the coast in one direction and five miles in the other, but they were not permitted to fish more than half a mile out from the shore.

In 1863 Mary Davis of St Mawes wrote a song to celebrate the very successful pilchard fishing season of 1862. An old newspaper cutting carries the report:

Little wonder that many wistful glances are cast backward over the past to the good old times when peace and plenty reigned supreme. The height of the prosperity of St Mawes was reached in the year 1862, in which year the men who were engaged on the seine boats received no less than £42 per man as the result of one enormous catch. The occasion was celebrated by great rejoicing and fixed the zeal of one local, Miss Mary Davies.

The great pilchard catch
By Mary Davies, St Mawes. January 1863
Late in the year of 62, the weather fine and gay, Our seiners jump'd onboard their boats and quickly row'd away, They got upon the fishing ground with out the least delay, Where many thousand pilchards round were sporting in the sea.

(chorus)
So success unto the Nelson seine,
The Diligence likewise
wazau, wazau, ye valiant men,
We give you all great praise.

Overboard our seine was quickly thrown, so merrily and gay, A thousand hogsheads we have stopped their colour's in the sea, Be quick, my lads, go stop the ends, and make them all secure, If Providence fine weather sends, we'll have them soon ashore.

(So success...)

We wrapped our seine so manfully a half a mile or more, Our capstans quickly did go round, soon brought us near shore, Seven grappling then we did let down to keep her in place, so come on lads we'll have a glass for now we hope she's safe.

(So success…)

A tucking now we must begin to Moon for flaskets run, A hundred hogsheads we must land before next rising sun, We landed them so carefully upon the cellar floor, Go call the girls of the town stand to the bulk once more.

(So success…)

Call Sally, Kitty, Peggy, Grace your crinolines put aside, For in the cellar you must come and there you must abide, Until our fish is bulked and packed and re-packed and back laid, Then a new dress and crinoline too for you will be well paid.

(So success…)

So now our fish is all broke out and barrell'd up so bright, Our merchants they will not forget to send them to the Straits, And may the year of '63, if Providence think right, Turn out so good as '62, to send another freight.

(So success…)

Here's a health our owners brave, the great expense they bore, There's Master James and Captain Green may blessings on them shower. Our children too will not forget the year of '62, it cloth'd their backs, shoe'd their feet, and filled their bellies too.

As with farmers and other tradespeople of the time, fishermen were obliged to pay tithes, or taxes, to the Church. These tithes were often paid in kind, the amount being one-tenth of the fisherman's catch or the farmer's harvest.

The Tithes Commutation Acts of 1836–60 made it law that all these tithes were to be in cash at a fixed amount.

The Cornish fishermen, who were generally very poor, bitterly resented having to hand over a tenth of their hard-earned catch. A survey carried out in 1836 shows that tithes were levied on the seine owners of St Mawes at £1 per seine, with the men who worked the nets having to pay a further 7s.7d. each, this amount being payable whether any fish were caught or not.

A court case in 1870 reveals that as one of the St Mawes seines was registered at Mevagissey, the vicar of that town was entitled to tithes from that net. The result of this case was that oil and salt belonging to the seine owners was seized and sold by auction to meet the vicar's demands. This, however, was not the end of the matter, as there were still the men's tithes to be accounted for.

The judge ruled that the seine owners, who had already paid the men their wages and a share of the catch, were liable for the men's tithes and that these they must pay to the vicar of Mevagissey.

The following year, the fishermen, although off to a good start, had a major setback. On 2 October, large shoals were seen off Pencarrow Roads. The Providence seine was shot but the weather took a turn for the worse and the men were forced to abandon the net and return to shore.

The following day they returned to find the seine still full of fish. The Stop & Go's seine, Enterprise, which had been shot under St Anthony lighthouse in the same conditions, however, was almost a total loss, and was only recovered in pieces.

A letter written by Mr Robert Snow of Falmouth, dated 9 March 1878, to the owners of the Adventure seine of St Mawes reveals:

The past season proved to be remarkably barren so far as the seine fishery was concerned, the total seine catch in the entire county being only 170 hogsheads. My expectations of a valuable catch were raised to an exceedingly high point more than once during the campaign; in fact, when making my rounds of inspection I saw an abundance of fish within a very short distance of Pendennis Point and very large quantities of fish were several times reported on the coast. Owing to an unfavourable state of tide or other unusual causes, the fish did not come within shooting ground; but the proximity to a successful result shows that my continued sanguine expectations have been well founded and strongly confirms my belief that perseverance must command the success which the enterprising adventurers so richly deserve.

In 1883 hopes were high at the prospect of setting up a pilchard-curing station at St Mawes to rival that at Mevagissey. In July, tanks and barrels began to arrive. The plan was abandoned soon afterwards, however, when it was published that the drift boats were to be charged a shilling for each landing. The charge at Falmouth at that time was only 1d. per 1,000, while at Plymouth each boat paid only a small sum for the whole season.

In the 1890s it was reported by the County Council Fishery Committee that the women who salted pilchards at Portscatho were still being paid in wool, with which they were expected to knit 'Guernseys' for their men-folk. At this time, the pilchard was still described as 'the most common food of the labouring poor'.

During the October storms of 1877 a huge quantity of pilchards found their way as far as Tolverne Reach – the oldest inhabitants at that time could not remember pilchards being found so far upriver. These fish had unfortunately escaped the notice of the huers at St Mawes and were taken up by some keen-eyed river men and sold on the quay at Truro.

In 1885, 15-year-old Lydia Davey of St Mawes wrote her poem, The Hobba:

'Twas on a day we'll all remember,
The second day of dull November,
Four watchers on the fishing ground,
Descried the Pilchards all around,
In haste, they then the HOBBA made,
One waved his jacket oe'r his head,
One tied a bag upon an oar
And waved it, shouting more and more,
While on the spot the seines to bring,
The fog bell now began to ring,
The men upon the quay were spying,
And Hobba's up they soon were crying.
Quickly the seiners did arrive,
Quickly the town was all alive,
Quickly the seines were rowed away,
While still the bag did madly sway.
The seiners pulled with might and main,
For fear the fish would float again,
Into deep water; but they found,
When they arrived upon the ground,
That in the turns they still were showing,
Their colour in the water glowing,
Without delay the seines were shot,
And three good schools within them caught.
With joyful speed their ends were fastened,
For swift to work the seiners hastened,
The grapnels laid, to keep them fast,
Then went ashore to have a glass;
For every work will better wag,
To the jingling of the money bag.
Soon as the daylight dawned around,
The dauntless tuckers sought the ground,
Mullion, where their seines were moored,
And, with importance, got aboard.
Soon in the tucks, lay all the lot,
Seething, and turning like a pot,
That's boiling; many came to view
The sight, both curious and new,
And happily in some hours more,
The fish lay on the cellar floor,
And all the women round about,
Were bulking; 'twas a curious rout,
The carpenter left board and mast,
The cobbler left his wax and last,
The brewer even left his malt
To go, and carry fish and salt.
Up to the eyes in Pilchard scales;
But merriment o'er all prevails.
Who cares for mud, or fishy smell?
The fish are in the bulk to sell;
Who cares for scales? They're glad they're sent,
For sixpences they represent.
So, when the girls do now dress fine,
You'll know it is the Pilchard shine.

Long life be to the owners brave,
And many more schools may they have,
And here's a health for all their pains,
Prosperity unto the seines
While to men, who worked so well,
Great praise is due, as all can tell.
Let's hope that all I am addressing,
Have thanked the Lord for his great blessing,
Who sent them to us, and then gave
Fine weather, all of them to save.
And may the year of Eighty-six,
If providence thinks right,
Be better still, than Eighty-five,
And send a larger freight.

In 1873 William Peters is recorded as a boatbuilder working in Polvarth, as is Peter Nicholas. Frederick Andrew was a registered pilot, along with William Dash, Joseph Dash, Joseph Vincent, James Tiddy and Samuel Lowry. John Dotson was carrying on his trade as a butcher and Green & Co. were busy as drapers, grocers and seine owners. Another butcher at this time was James Pomeroy. There seems to have been no shortage of shops in the village, with Miss Blanch Collins, Robert Dash, John Hancock, Mary Jane, Mrs Jane Libby, Mrs Mary Lower, William Snow, Ann Maria Thomas and Mrs Jane Vincent all opening their doors to supply the residents of St Mawes with provisions. And if you needed new ropes, then Edward Hitchins was your man.

The season of 1899 was hailed as a complete disaster, a local paper carrying the report:

The seine boats which, for several months, have ridden at their moorings opposite the quay, carrying their nets, kedges and tackling of all kinds, ready for the fray, have at length been relieved of their burdens. The gear has been stowed in the sheds and the boats taken up to Polvarth, to await the commencement of another season and, it is to be hoped, a more successful one. This season has been, unfortunately, a complete failure. 'Nat wan fish' has been caught. One net, only, having been shot for the season and that, more's the pity, was in vain.

At St Mawes, during the heavy gale which raged on Tuesday morning that same week, two seine boats had broken from their moorings, one off the pier belonging to Messrs Collins and the other at Polvarth, belonging to Mr C. Pascoe of St Just. Fortunately, in both cases, no damage was done. A good number of men turned out and, with many willing hands, soon got the seine out of the former, and with ropes pulled her into the pier. Seven years later the *Hope* seine boat, owned by Mr. R. Collins of St Mawes, broke from her moorings during a gale and was driven onto the rocks at Bohella. Her nets were washed away through holes made by the rocks. Two years before a similar accident had befallen the *Vollyer*, attached to the same seine boat.

Leslie Green, Tommy Green and Jimmy Green sorting oysters, c.1930.

That same winter, 1905, Mr Hancock's seine boat and one of the steamers became the victims of rough weather.

During the heavy gale on Saturday night and early Sunday morning, the Onward *seine boat, belonging to J. Hancock & Co., broke away from her mooring and got stranded on Polvarth beach. Fortunately no damage was done and, with the flowing tide, she was got off. About eight o'clock, a boat belonging to the Steam Packet Co. broke adrift and was cast onto the rocks. But owing to the promptness of E. Thomas and others, it was saved.*

On 9 October 1913, a reporter in the *Cornish Echo* wrote that the fishermen at St Mawes were having a very poor season:

For some time, the fishermen have been daily eagerly hoping that either the huer, or someone else, would discover a shoal of pilchards sufficiently large for the four seines to shoot, but so far this season no fish have been landed by the seines. The cry of Hobba! Hobba! called many of the fishermen in haste from their homes about four 4 o'clock on Saturday morning and, on it being reported that a large shoal of pilchards had been seen some distance off the village, the four seiners put out. But the fish which had been seen jumping out of the water, proved to be too far at sea for the seines to be shot.

Things were little better at Portloe, although by this time they had turned their attention to drift fishing, which meant that instead of them waiting for the shoals to come close inshore, they could fish in much deeper water. This tiny village was almost completely dependent on fishing, as can be seen from the number of boats employed there, and a bad season must have brought severe hardship to many of the inhabitants:

As far as the twenty-six drift boats working out from Portloe are concerned, the present pilchard season is stated to be the worst on record. The highest catch this season has been about 2,000 compared with 13,000 last year and the catches have averaged from 500 to 200 fish, against an average of about 5,000 each boat on many nights last year. The price obtained for the few catches landed has been good, having risen from 20s. to about 30s. per thousand.

Over in Portscatho the fishermen had had a slightly better week:

The drift pilchard fishing has shown a slight improvement at Portscatho. Better catches than previously obtained during the season were landed on Thursday night. On Friday night, the highest take of the season, one of 5,300, was made and with the exception of one, all the boats caught 1,500 and over.
The other boat secured only 250. This season's record,

Top and above: *Joe Dotson's boat, the* Alberta.

however, does not compare favourably with that of last year, which exceeded 10,000. The fishing on Saturday night resulted in catches of 2,200. Four boats put out on Sunday night and averaged about one hundred fish each. The good price of 26s.6d. per thousand is being realised.

By the following year, 1914, it was 'all over bar the shouting', as we say. It was reported that, unless some extraordinary takes of pilchard occurred, the pilchard fishery was faced with a very serious outlook. Unfortunately, the pilchards failed to show themselves and within a matter of weeks, all minds were occupied with a far worse problem – Britain was at war with Germany.

As we have already established, most of the local men looked to the sea for their employment. A survey drawn up at the end of the eighteen hundreds found that out of 66 local businessmen, 18 were engaged as river or harbour pilots; seven were skippers, three were boatbuilders; two were ship-wrights and one was a rope maker, working at the Rope Walk.

Back in 1854 the men of St Mawes had been called to the quay and asked by Captain Sheringham of the Royal Navy to join the new Coastguard service. He told them that there was a great need for them to join, as their country's defence depended on it. Those who made the pledge would be expected to make themselves available for gunnery training for 28 days each year. In all, 10,000 men around the coast of Britain were signed up.

The *West Briton* published an article in 1889 concerning the funeral of a St Mawes fisherman. This report sheds much light on old St Mawes, and in particular the great esteem in which the local fishermen were held as singers. In those days, the mourners would follow the coffin on foot to the churchyard at St Just, often singing all the way:

Did you ever hear the Cornish fishermen sing? Not in Church or chapel but outside, with the blue dome of heaven for their roof and in sight of the grand ocean, within sound of its thundering surf or its rippling wavelets. If not, you have missed a treat. It is magnif-icent. They seem to give full vent to the music that is born with them and do it too with an unconscious simplicity that clothes it with grandeur, comparable only with the rugged magnificence with which Dame Nature has endowed the crag bound coast amid which they are cradled.

I enjoyed the pleasure of listening to such an Anthem on Sunday last and, although the occasion was sad, one could not but feel a throb of real delight as the voices mingled with the music of the waves in perfect harmony. Near by, a white haired fisherman, book in

hand, read in clear ringing tones the first verse of that beautiful hymn, 'Safe in the Arms of Jesus'. As the sad procession wended its way to the quiet Churchyard, one of the oldest fishermen in the town approached me and said, 'Now you see a real St Mawes funeral, 'tis the first you ever saw I'll be bound. Now you see the feelings and the sympathies of the people. Every funeral used to be like this in times gone by.'

Celebration Bonfires at St Mawes

At the news that Lord Kitchener's Army had been successful in the taking of Ladysmith, which victory heralded the end to the Boer War in 1902, there were great celebrations in St Mawes. It was reported in a local paper:

Seldom, has such a wave of patriotism swept over the village as when the news of the relief of Ladysmith was received on Thursday. Ringing cheers rent the air from the old and young alike. All available space was deco-rated with bunting and in the evening, the fife and drum band paraded the streets playing patriotic airs.

Mr Spargoe James had two immense bonfires ignited and finally set fire to a warren near the Castle, this giving a grand effect. Another bonfire was lit on the pier head and it was well nigh on midnight before the village assumed its wonted serenity.

By 1914, although the local trades were still apparent, things were moving forward. Edwin Adams, John Dash, Eleanor Bennetto, Mehalah Collins, James Green, Charles Harris and Emma and Hettie Tiddy were all renting out apartments, while Philip Johnson was running a boarding-house.

The boatbuilders were still busy, with Nicholas Peters and Henry Theodore German plying their trade. The Andain brothers, George Collins, Robert Dash (whose premises were next to the St Mawes Hotel), William Green and William Jenkin were all running their grocery businesses. while Lewis Cock, also a grocer, doubled as the deputy harbourmaster.

Crew of the No.10 pilot boat, with pilots John Sawle, Charles Fittock, Freddie Watts and Charles Jenkin and crew members Charlie Andrew, Richard German and Johnnie Pascoe.

An unidentified pilot boat off St Mawes.

CHAPTER 9

Piloting

Charlie Jenkins was one of the crew of the No.10 pilot boat, which, with others, had her moorings off St Mawes on the St Anthony side of the river. The crew of the No.10 were Harry Green, John Sawle, Charlie Fittock, Fred Watts, Charlie Jenkin, Johnnie Pascoe, Richard (Dick) German – who was my great grandfather – and Tom Jenkins.

The registration number of the boats changed through the years, as in her launch year she was registered No. 9.

Initially described as 58 feet long and named the *Richard Green*, she was built in 1866:

On Saturday there was launched at Mr. Trethowan's shipyard, Little Falmouth, a handsomely modelled pilot cutter of 46 tons OM [Old Measurement, or builders' measure]. *She is the property of Messrs R. Green & Co., of St Mawes, and is expected to sail fast, and be a good sea boat.*

When first registered her owners were listed as Richard Green, pilot; William Green, fisherman; Ann Nancarrow, spinster; and James Gordon Watts, ship owner.

Richard Green, her principal owner, after whom she was named, was born in St Mawes in 1823, and is first listed as a Falmouth pilot in 1854, being taken off the list in 1870.

On 26 October 1875 the *Richard Green* was re-registered at Falmouth Custom House as No.19 in that year, when her length was given as 65.7 feet, as opposed to the 58 feet in her former register. Like several other pilot cutters at about this time, she had been lengthened by over seven feet, to give more accommodation space for the pilots, and possibly to improve her sea-keeping abilities.

At the time when the *Richard Green* was built, the pilotage business for the port of Falmouth was a very competitive, cut-throat affair, with boats racing each other in the Channel for the job of piloting in home-ward-bound ships. The outward pilotage usually lay with the pilot who had first brought the ship in. Highest prized and the most challenging to the pilots were the deep-sea sailing vessels bound for 'Falmouth for Orders' after many months or even years away from home.

Such competition naturally gave rise to all-too-frequent near-miss situations, where one boat tried to cut another out by driving between a rival cutter and her intended prize – the prize, of course, being the fees for bringing that ship safely to anchorage within the harbour limits. Occasionally there were heavy collisions, leaving the cutters badly damaged or even sunk. Even without such cut-throat competition there was always the risk of being run down in fog or a heavy sea, as the cutters attempted to put their pilots aboard a homeward-bound ship in the open Channel off the Lizard.

In addition to the occupational rivalry between

Rose German with her mother Ellen, who used to watch for the No. 10 pilot boat to return to her moorings so that she could prepare a meal for her husband Richard.

individual pilot boats, there was highly competitive local rivalry between the St Mawes and Falmouth men. This competitive nature was reflected in their play, and nowhere more so than in the pilot boat races at the annual regattas. These were lively affairs, slightly reckless at times, and were usually accompanied by heavy drinking sessions – though not until the race was won or lost.

In 1887, as a result of bigger and faster steamships taking over from the sailing vessels, the Falmouth and District Pilot Boat Association was formed. The pilots now agreed to work co-operatively and it was resolved to bring all the cutters into joint ownership. By this time the *Richard Green* was registered as No.10, with shareholders listed as Olivia Green, Mrs Green and Michael William Beckford.

The F&D PBA, for reasons known only to themselves, refused to loan the boat to the St Mawes Regatta committee in 1888. Although we assume that she was seaworthy, as she was still registered, she had been in trouble the previous summer:

The No. 10 pilot cutter, Richard Green, was greatly damaged on Thursday evening. On account of the

rough weather she anchored in Helford Sound. The gale increased during the night, and between four and five yesterday morning she was driven from her anchorage and went ashore on the rocks, and it is feared that she is a total wreck. The crew of seven men, who were on board her, escaped in the small boat attached to her.

The four pilots and three apprentices on board that night, all from St Mawes, were W. Jenkin, J. Scott, Fredrick Hancock, Charles Jenkin, Alfred Pascoe, Charles Greet and Joseph Green.

She was, however, not a total loss, as she continued in service until 1917. The following year it was recorded that: 'Richard Green, cancelled and registry closed this 15\3\1918. Vessel broken up.'

Although the *Richard Green* is well documented, St Mawes men were already employed in pilot work before she was built.

In 1776 those listed were Charles Green, seaman; Ambrose Green, seaman; Frederick Hancock, pilot; Richard Andrew, pilot; Charles Bickford, seaman; George Bickford, apprentice and Nicholas Bickford, master.

In Loving Memory

OF

EDWARD JAMES,

Beloved Husband of ADELAIDE HODGE, and late Trinity Pilot, of St. Mawes,

Who passed away on December 27th, 1915,

AGED 65 YEARS.

———

Funeral will leave the house at 2 p.m. on Wednesday, December 29th, for St. Just Churchyard.

St Mawes

St Mawes

CHAPTER 10

War Times

St Mawes Sapper's Narrow Escape

Sapper Fleetwood German, of the Royal Engineers, son of Mr. and Mrs. Richard J. German, of St Mawes, is now visiting his parents, having been granted eight day's leave. He has spent eleven months in France with the 11th Company, Royal Engineers, and has seen plenty of fighting at La Bassee and Givanche. He witnessed the grand charge of the Irish Guards when Sergeant O'Leary won his VC, also the capture of three lines of German trenches at Richburg. Sapper German took part in the operations at Loos and at Vermellies.

The work of the Royal Engineers has been of a varied character, including the erection of barbed wire, the repairing of trenches, the consolidation of positions, etc and sometimes it has to be carried out under very trying circumstances. So far, Sapper German has come through the war without a scratch. On one occasion he had a very narrow escape, for a bullet passed through the wrinkled sleeve of his tunic, just near the elbow, without touching the arm.

Fleetwood wrote to his sister in St Mawes in 1916 from Rouen in France:

Dear Ellen,

Just a line to say I received your letter alright. Glad to hear that you were all quite well at home as I am pleased to say it leaves me pretty fair at the time of writing. I am shifting further up the line again in a day or so. I think you had better wait until you hear from me again before you write another. As soon as we get to the other place I will write and let you know the address. Conclude with love to all at home including yourself. From Fleet.

Fleetwood German died from wounds received at High Wood, Somme, in France, on 21 August 1916, aged 23. In 1915 a local newspaper reported that, 'the name of A.V. Jenkins RFR has appeared in the list of wounded on HMS *Albion*. On Monday Mrs Charles Jenkins of Bohilla, St Mawes, received the letter from the secretary of the Admiralty:

I regret to inform you that telegraphic information has

In Ever-loving Memory

OF

ISAAC FLEETWOOD GREEN

(Lance Corporal, Royal Engineers),

Beloved second Son of RICHARD and ELLEN GERMAN,
Rope Walk, St. Mawes,

Who died of wounds received at High Wood, Somme, France, AUGUST 21st, 1916,

AGED 23 YEARS AND 4 MONTHS.

———

" Rest in Peace."

Fleetwood German, who was killed on 21 August 1916 at the Battle of the Somme, aged 23.

been received that Albert Victor Jenkins, able seaman, RFR of HMS Albion was wounded in action on the 18th inst. No particulars as to the nature of the injuries have been received but on receipt of such information you will again be communicated with.

Albert had joined the Navy as a boy and left the service when he was 22 years old, passing into the Fleet Reserve. He went to America and Canada and returned to St Mawes to undertake his annual training. When the war started he was called up and drafted to the *Albion*.

Like all communities, St Mawes and St Just lost a number of young men in the First World War. They were: James Benny, Harry Blight, J.A. Blitchford, R.J. Blitchford, T. Christiania, William Cocking, W.L. Clode, A.J. Dobson, J. Edwards, W. Edwards, Fleetwood German, Theodore German, Irving Green,

Joe Dotson Royal Naval Reserve in the 1914-18 war.

R.H. Harris, Sidney Hearne, E. Jenking, E.A. Kendall, A.J. Lawrence, Jas Lelean, John Michell, Nicholls Odgers, Edward Peel, Richard Preston, Ernest Sparkes, J.W. Thomas, S.J. Tiddy and R. Trevarthan.

The loss of these 27 men from a relatively small community must have affected almost every family in the parish.

Just 23 years later, the country was once more at war with Germany and, as a result, many thousands of troops swelled the population of the Roseland, especially in the long run-up to D-Day. Falmouth, with its docks, was a constant target for German bombers, and gun emplacements were installed at St Mawes and St Anthony.

In 1941 the motor vessel *Joma* was struck by a mine while she was on St Mawes bank adjusting her

No. 14693

R V 8.

CERTIFICATE OF DISCHARGE
FROM THE ROYAL NAVAL RESERVE FORCE.

ISSUED BY ADMIRALTY AND BOARD OF TRADE.

1132 [859/60]   Printed by W. P. Griffith & Sons, Ld., Prujean Square, Old Bailey, London, E.C.   11/00v

Surname of Reserve Man	Christian Name of Reserve Man	Certificate R V 2	
		Number	Letter
Dotson	*Joseph James*	*1983*	*H.*

Date of joining Reserve	Rating on Discharge	Grounds of Discharge
12 Dec. 1890.	*Trained Man Second Class R N R*	*Completion on the 12 Dec. 1900, of ten years' service*

THIS IS TO CERTIFY, That the Naval Reserve Man above named has ~~this day~~ been discharged from the Royal Naval Reserve Force, as above stated

Signed this *24th* day of *September 1901.*

By Order of the Lords Commissioners of the Admiralty and the Lords of the Committee of Privy Council for Trade.

Registrar-General of Shipping and Seamen.

Joe Dotson's certificate of Discharge from the Royal Naval Reserve, 1901..

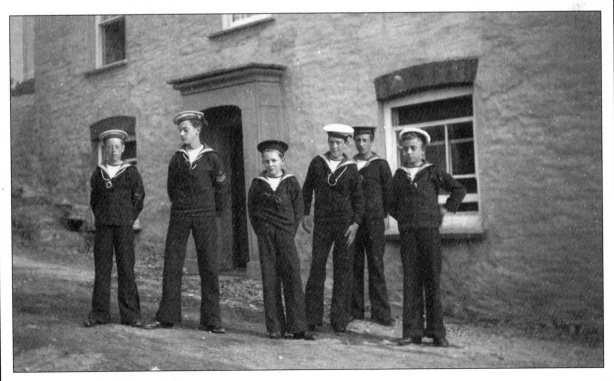

Local sailor boys show off their new uniforms, c.1940.

THE UNVEILING OF ST. MAWES WAR-MEMORIAL, OCT. 17, 1921.

1

All people that on earth do dwell,
  Sing to the Lord with cheerful voice ;
Him serve with mirth, His praise forth
  tell :
Come ye before Him and rejoice.

The Lord, ye know, is God indeed ;
Without our aid he did us make ;
We are his flock, He doth us feed,
And for His sheep he doth us take.

O enter, then, His gates with praise,
  Approach with joy His courts unto ;
Praise, laud, and bless His name always,
For it is seemly so to do.

For why : the Lord our God is good,
His mercy is for ever sure,
His truth at all times firmly stood,
And shall from age to age endure.

ADDRESS.

SECRETARY'S STATEMENT.

THE LORD LIEUTENANT.

CHILDREN'S WREATH.

HYMN 2.   PRAYER.

LESSON.   BRIEF ADDRESS.

HYMN 3.   BENEDICTION.

VOTE OF THANKS.
GOD SAVE THE KING.

2

O God, our help in ages past,
  Our hope for years to come,
Our shelter from the stormy blast,
  And our eternal home.

Under the shadow of Thy throne
  Thy saints have dwelt secure :
Sufficient is Thine arm alone,
  And our defence is sure.

Before the hills in order stood,
  Or earth received her frame,
From everlasting Thou art God,
  To endless years the same.

A thousand ages in Thy sight
  Are like an evening gone ;
Short as the watch that ends the night
  Before the rising sun.

The busy tribes of flesh and blood
  With all their toils and fears,
Are carried downwards by the flood,
  And lost in following years,

O God, our help in ages past,
  Our hope for years to come,
Be Thou our guard while troubles last,
  And our eternal home.

3

Jerusalem the golden !
  With milk and honey blest !
Beneath thy contemplation
  Sink heart and voice oppressed.
I know not, oh ! I know not,
  What joys await us there,
What radiancy of glory,
  What bliss beyond compare !

They stand, those halls of Zion,
  All jubilant with song,
And bright with many an angel
  And all the martyr-throng ;
The Prince is ever in them ;
  The daylight is serene ;
The pastures of the blessed
  Are decked in glorious sheen.

There is the throne of David,
  And there, from care released,
The shout of them that triumph,
  The song of them that feast.
And they who with their Leader
  Have conquered in the fight,

Emma Adeline Sawle, c.1914.

Stanley Ferris during the Second World War.

compass. Three of her gunners were killed and six others injured. On 23 October 1943 an American Liberator aircraft crashed near St Mawes, killing her crew of 11.

In the war, we used to keep the fire engine up the Brake Yard just below the school. One night we was just *getting aboard when a German fighter came over flying parallel with the road. He started to fire and we had no time to run for cover. The doors of the engine were peppered with bullet holes and Jack got hit in the leg. Someone ran down the hill and fetched his missus and she came running up. 'Thank God,' she said. 'Thank God I made 'un change 'is under clothes this morning.'*

The steamer Alexandra *arrives at the quay alongside a ketch carrying coal, c.1900.*

The steamer Alexandra *on her way to Falmouth.*

CHAPTER 11

Steamers

By far the most pleasurable way to reach St Mawes, or indeed to leave it, is by water, and although many locals and visitors alike have their own crafts, the regular sailings of the passenger boats have, for many years, been a very important lifeline to the village. These regular ferry crossings were not available until 1869. Before that it was a far more chancy matter, as this old yarn tells us.

We were bound for Penryn and as we passed Castle Point Billy remarked; 'Did you ever hear the story of Henry and Uncle Jan.' On my replying in the negative, Billy settled himself in a comfortable corner and prepared to tell his tale, which was as follows: Many years ago, before the steamers ran between Falmouth and St Mawes, and before the big bell at the lighthouse sounded its warning notes over the waters of the harbour, Henry and Uncle Jan were engaged by a gentleman to carry him from St Mawes to Falmouth. It was a foggy afternoon; the mists hung thickly over the water, and as they were about to put off a friend suggested that a compass would be handy, and volun-

teered to lend one. His offer was accepted, and they started on their perilous journey. All went well until they reached St Mawes Castle Point. At this juncture Henry said; 'I'll pull the paddles, Uncle Jan, and you steer.' Placing the compass on the thwarts, Uncle Jan sat down and watched it.

Henry plied the oars. 'How's her head, Uncle Jan?' he asked. 'Nor-Nor West' replied Uncle Jan. 'Well keep her

Top right and above: *One of the early steamers, possibly the* Alexandra.

Joe, Ellen and Muriel Dotson, 1918.

up,' answered Henry. Another long pull and again Henry sung out; 'How's her head Uncle Jan?'

'Nor Nor West,' he answered again. 'Well keep her well up, the tide is going out.'

Henry strained every nerve, and at length, after about a couple of hours the old man cried out gleefully; 'I can see a light Henry, we've made a good land fall, it's Kill-kee.'

Through the gloom they managed, after some trouble, to find a landing place, jumped on shore and found themselves, after two hours' hard pulling, at Percuil. The language used by all three was not exactly Parliamentary, especially when on a closer examination of the compass they found that the needle was jammed and unable to move. They were so upset by the discovery that they turned into the then flourishing inn which stood at the ferry, where they made a night of it. On reaching Falmouth the next day they landed their passenger and returned to St Mawes well out of pocket.

In August 1869 Ezekiel Tucker, William Jenkin and Frederick Andrew joined forces with William Henry Williams, a merchant from London, to purchase the *Wotton*, an iron screw tug formerly owned by Howard and Robert Fox, who had established the first passenger ferry service between Percuil, St Mawes and Falmouth. The St Mawes Steam Tug &

Passenger Co. Ltd was formally founded in 1872. By 1878 Edward Hancock had sold his shares in the wooden screw steamer *Jane* to the St Mawes company. Among the members of the company were William Rowe of Falmouth and Edwin Hicks of St Mawes, both of whom would go on to be chairmen of the company.

When Ezekiel Tucker died in 1889, his shares in the *Wotton* were purchased by Edwin Hicks. William Jenkin's son, Edward who lived at Roseland Cottage, St Mawes, became master of the *Alexandra*, and in 1917 was appointed managing owner of all the company's vessels.

Early in 1886 the company had the *Roseland* built by Cox & Co. of Falmouth. Of steel construction, she boasted triple expansion engines and two saloons to provide shelter in rough weather. William Jenkin was appointed the first master of the vessel, which would go on to ferry passengers in her home waters for the next 50 years.

The St Mawes company did not have the transport of passengers and goods to themselves for long. In 1887 the Roseland & Falmouth Steam Packet Co. Ltd was formed to provide a steamer service to and from Falmouth.

The first boat employed was the *St Mawes Castle*, built by Harvey's of Hayle. Her skipper was Richard

William Jenkin, aged 100, in 1925.

Joe Dotson, with the steamboat office and waiting-room in the back-ground.

Samuel Collins, who lived at Albert Terrace, St Mawes. The *St Mawes Castle* was sold in 1897 to a West Australian steam company. She never reached her new home, however, as she sank in the Indian Ocean.

With the roads of the Roseland peninsula still in a very rough state, the steamers were an ideal form of transport for the Royal Mails entering and leaving St Mawes. This twice-daily subsidised service enabled the St Mawes Steam Tug & Passenger Co., bearing the RMS sign, to operate year round.

In 1894 the newly built *Princess May* was brought into service. With her more luxurious below-deck saloons and seating, and carrying a raised poop deck, she embarked on a full programme of scenic trips, including a two-hour visit to Portscatho or the Helford River, Portloe, Mevagissey and St Just in Roseland, where passengers could enjoy an hour looking around the churchyard.

Eight years later, when the *Princess May* was sold and sailed to South Africa, she was replaced by the *Alexandra*. This new vessel gave good service for the next 14 years and in 1916 was acquired by the War Ministry.

The St Mawes Steamship Co., the chairman of which was Edwin Hicks, ran the St Mawes, *the* Roseland, *the motor launch* Berry Castle *and the* St Gerrans. *The skippers were Ben Johns, Jim Tiddy and Fred Ferris. I remember*

two of the engineers, Uncle Mathew Sawle and Bill Barnicoat.

These boats played a very important part in the life of the village, as virtually everything was brought in and taken out by steamer. The first boat in the mornings left at 7a.m to take workers to Falmouth docks and the schoolchildren to Falmouth Grammar School and Falmouth High School for girls.

The St Mawes, *which had an upper deck and large covered cabin area, operated trips to the Lizard and Fowey. On these trips they had to carry a qualified captain and engineer. Uncle Harold Watts, being an ex RN Lieutenant Engineer, went on these and I usually went with him.*

Charlie Dash was the man who, when the tide was out, rowed the passengers ashore. He also delivered the parcels which arrived on the steamer.

The sale price of the Princess May, *one of the St Mawes excursion steamers which has been disposed of to a company for service in South Africa, was £2,600. The statement that the* SS Victoria *has been sold is premature, the terms of sale not having been agreed upon.*

The *Alexandra*, the *May Queen*, the *Roseland*, the *Resilient* and the *St Gerrans*, among others, have all ploughed their way through good weather and bad

St Mawes pier in the 1930s. On the quay bags of coal awaiting collection. The schooner has just delivered road stone from Mousehole, and sitting at her mooring is the Pet, which was used to carry building materials to St Mawes from Falmouth.

St Mawes c.1930, when new houses were beginning to appear.

Top and above: Joe Dotson aboard his boat **Alberta** *with a party of holiday-makers, c.1930.*

Millwood Cottage in the 1940s.

Millwood being re-roofed 1950s.

St Mawes in the early days of motor transport, with more goods and people beginning to arrive by road.

Coal being collected by horse and cart in the 1940s.

Pictured in the 1940s (foreground) is the houseboat Rover, *a converted First World War MTB.*

Passengers await the arrival of the steamer in 1958.

An unidentified steamer arrives at the quay in the 1950s.

to keep this important service running. In April 1888 it was advertised that:

The Truro Mercantile Association have entered into an arrangement with the owners of the Resolute, *and that steamer will now run regularly every Wednesday, starting from Percuil at nine o'clock in the morning, calling at St Mawes, St Just, King Harry, Tolverne and Malpas. The very moderate return fare of 1 shilling from St Mawes to Truro and back is charged. Arrangements have also been made that, in case the steamer should not be able to reach Truro Quay, a waggonette will meet the steamer at Malpas every Wednesday for a return fare of 4d.*

The arrival of the new steamship *St Gerrans* caused a great deal of excitement in the Roseland, as she was of the latest design and the first of her kind in this part of the country.

In 1927 she was brought into service and caused quite a stir locally. She was licensed to carry 280 passengers within the limits of Falmouth Harbour and 168 on coastal trips within the limits of the Dodman and Black Head.

The Public, generally in Falmouth, St Mawes and district, will be interested to know that in the first week in August, the enterprising and progressive St Mawes Steamship Company will have launched a new excursion ship which will undoubtedly be one of the finest of its kind in the country. Apart from the residents in the district, there are thousands of visitors who greatly

enjoy the trips, run from Falmouth to St Mawes, Percuil and St Anthony, and the latter are most astounded at the moderate fares charged when compared with many other seaside places in the country.

The new steamer is to be named the St Gerrans *and, no doubt, the residents of that historic village will, in consequence, have more than a passing interest in the craft, just as the inhabitants of St Mawes have in the sister ship, the* St Mawes.

Constructed of steel, she has teak decks and fittings and two light masts. It is interesting to note that the boat is a new type, being the first of her kind in the West. She has a saloon upper deck, fitted with tram car seats.

There is a general saloon aft, which includes a gentlemen's lavatory, nicely fitted out, with wash basin, mirrors, etc., whilst on the fore side of the engine room is a ladies' cabin similarly fitted.

Both cabins are fitted with steel stoves and coal will be used. It can thus be seen that the Company are anxious to provide warmth for their passengers during the winter months.

The *St Gerrans* along with the *Roseland* and the *St Mawes*, were joined in the mid-1930s by the small wooden motor launch *Berry Castle*.

In 1938 yet another steamer was purchased. The *Royal Jubilee* was brought down from Bridlington and promptly renamed the *New Roseland*. World events, however, were about to disrupt the peaceful ferry journeys. Along with the *St Mawes*, the *New Roseland* and the *St Gerrans* were acquired by the War

The St Mawes ferry, 2006.

Ministry. The *St Mawes* was immediately sent up to the Clyde to provide transport for troops. The *New Roseland* was sent up to Devonport to replace the *St Gerrans*, which had experienced engine problems.

The original *Roseland* ended her days as a houseboat and was often seen around the local creeks.

Capt Ben Johns, a familiar sight on the *St Gerrans*, was her skipper for many years. Ben was born in Portloe on 1 June 1883 and volunteered for the Royal Navy on 26 April 1901. His papers state that he volunteered for a period of 12 years and that he had been brought up in the trade of 'fisher lad'.

This 12-year period was quickly succeeded by the First World War, and so we find leading seaman Johns commencing War Service on 26 July 1915 and remaining in the Royal Navy until 1921.

Uncle Ben was a deck hand in old man Jenkin's time. I can remember them putting what we always called the cow shed in the stern of the old Roseland, *so that there was somewhere to shelter. Before then, if it was bad weather, you just to put up with it.*

The St Just and St Mawes parish magazine of June 1965 reported:

On March 3 we laid to rest Capt. Ben Johns, who had

reached the very good age of 83 years. A Church member of long standing, Capt. Ben was on the Church Council for many years and a sidesman at St Mawes. Most of you will know of his service to the Royal Navy and of his long connection with the Steamship Company and with the local branch of the British Legion.

In December 1967 the *Falmouth Packet* carried the headline, 'Hovercraft service for St Mawes. The St Mawes Steam Tug & Passenger Co. had been sold to three London businessmen and one member of the old board. The article went on to say that of the four boats serving St Mawes, the *Princess Maud* had undergone a conversion to an 'all-weather' vessel. The new board of directors said the they would be looking at ways of 'maintaining and streamlining the service'. For some months there had been speculation that a hovercraft service was to be introduced. Mr Trelore of the board stated that these rumours were 'not without some foundation'. He went on to point out that if such a service was introduced it would cut the travelling time between St Mawes and Falmouth to four minutes.

Thankfully, the hovercraft service, like the Roseland railway, never materialised, or the tranquillity of the river would have been lost forever.

CHAPTER 12

Schooldays

On 20 October 1887 the *West Briton* published a letter from a very concerned local, who reported on the sad neglect at St Just School of the children's welfare .

Sir, I deem it my duty, in the cause of humanity, to appeal through the medium of the Press to the parties concerned and responsible for cruel neglect of the usual and paid-for coal supply for the proper timing at the school at St Just in Roseland.

The children stand or sit, trembling with the cold for several hours daily. The school being built upon the top of a hill and the school being too small for the duties thereof, necessitates one part of its duties being performed in the porch and the condition of the children is thus rendered dreadfully disagreeable and indeed dangerous to health.

Ten years later St Mawes Board School seems to have a much more socially aware atmosphere.

On 24 June 1897 13-year-old St Mawes schoolgirl Ellen German wrote:

As everyone knows on Tuesday it was the Jubilee. All over the British Empire the Diamond Jubilee was kept up. Sunday was the day of Victoria's accession but the celebration was not had until Tuesday. In London they had beautiful weather but I am going to tell you about the celebration in our parish. The children went down on the quay early, and about a quarter to two the medals were given away, all the children who were there had medals. After this we formed a procession and marched up the parade, the ministers went first, then came the band after this came the big and small boys, then the girls and behind the women. We went into J.C. Kennerlly Esq's ground and there sang a verse of the National Anthem. Then we went up around Castle Lane and went into the Jubilee field. When we got in the sports began. I was not there to see the first two races but I was there to see the rest. At half past four the children had their tea, and a good tea I had. After this the grown up people had their tea, and the games continued until eight o'clock. About this time it was damp and foggy and many people went home for their jackets. Many young people stayed there and played two's and three's until 9 o'clock. About ten o'clock a big bonfire was lit and we had to keep a good way from it, we could see one at Pendennis Castle and several in other places. When I got home it was eleven o'clock and I was very tired. After having my supper I went to bed wishing we had a holiday again the next day.

In September of that same year Ellen recorded for posterity a typical day at St Mawes School:

Yesterday I came to school at 9 o'clock and we went into our places. Then the early ones were marked, after this Master read a portion of Scripture. This being done we said the Lord's Prayer, and then bade Master good morning and then began our lessons. The first lesson was arithmetic, standard seven had stocks, I had all mine right. The next lesson was dictation. I did not have any mistakes so we were sent out to play. We had about a quarter of an hour for play, then the bell rang and we came in again. The lesson was poetry, it was an extract from The Deserted Village *by Oliver Goldsmith. The last lesson was transcription we had to write off a piece of our poetry from the board, and if we could not tell it after twelve we had to stay in and learn it. Anyhow I learnt mine and went in good time. When I got home my dinner was not ready so I took my little sister for a walk. When we got home my dinner was ready and I sat down and enjoyed a good meal. This being over I fetched a turn of water and then came to school in good time. It was sewing in the afternoon so I took my work and went to my place. I am making a nightdress for my examination work so you see I am very busy. At half past four we went home. I had my tea and then went for some errands. After I had fetched them I did my knitting and about 9 o'clock I went to bed.*

She also recorded that the children had broken up from school on 30 July until 30 August:

… so that was a long time to enjoy ourselves. The first week we had friends from Falmouth so I had plenty to do. The second week I was busy fetching beach for the path but I do not like doing it.

Living in a small cottage on Grove Terrace with a wife and six children to feed, Richard German, although employed as a pilot, had little choice but to find time to grow what food he could in his garden. Ellen wrote that although it was:

… not very large we have one piece of ground on the north side and one on the south. In the back garden we have cabbages, shallots, onions and kidney beans, and in another place Father had got seeds in but they are up now, there are broccoli, savoy and leeks. Father has also tilled savoy in the back garden and he will soon be tilling out the leeks. In the front garden we have got a

Top and above: *St Mawes infants, c.1900.*

Schedule No.

Standard 6.

Examination Paper.

Name of School *Board St Mawes*

Name of Pupil *Ellen A German*

Dictation. *Nov 17, 1896.*

SCHOLASTIC TRADING CO., LTD., BRISTOL.

So with our youths. We once taught them to make Latin verses, and called them educated; now we teach them to leap and to row, to hit a ball with a bat, and called call them educated. Can they plough, can they sow, can they plant at the right time, or build with a steady hand? Is it the effect of their lives to be chaste, knightly, faithful, holy in thought, lovely in word and deed? This it is to be truly educated.

It is my steady so wish that school boys should learn skill in ploughing and seamanship rather than in (cricket) cricket; and that young ladies should often be sent to help the cook and housemaid, when they would rather be playing tennis.

Ellen German's dictation paper, 1896.

St Mawes School, c.1900.

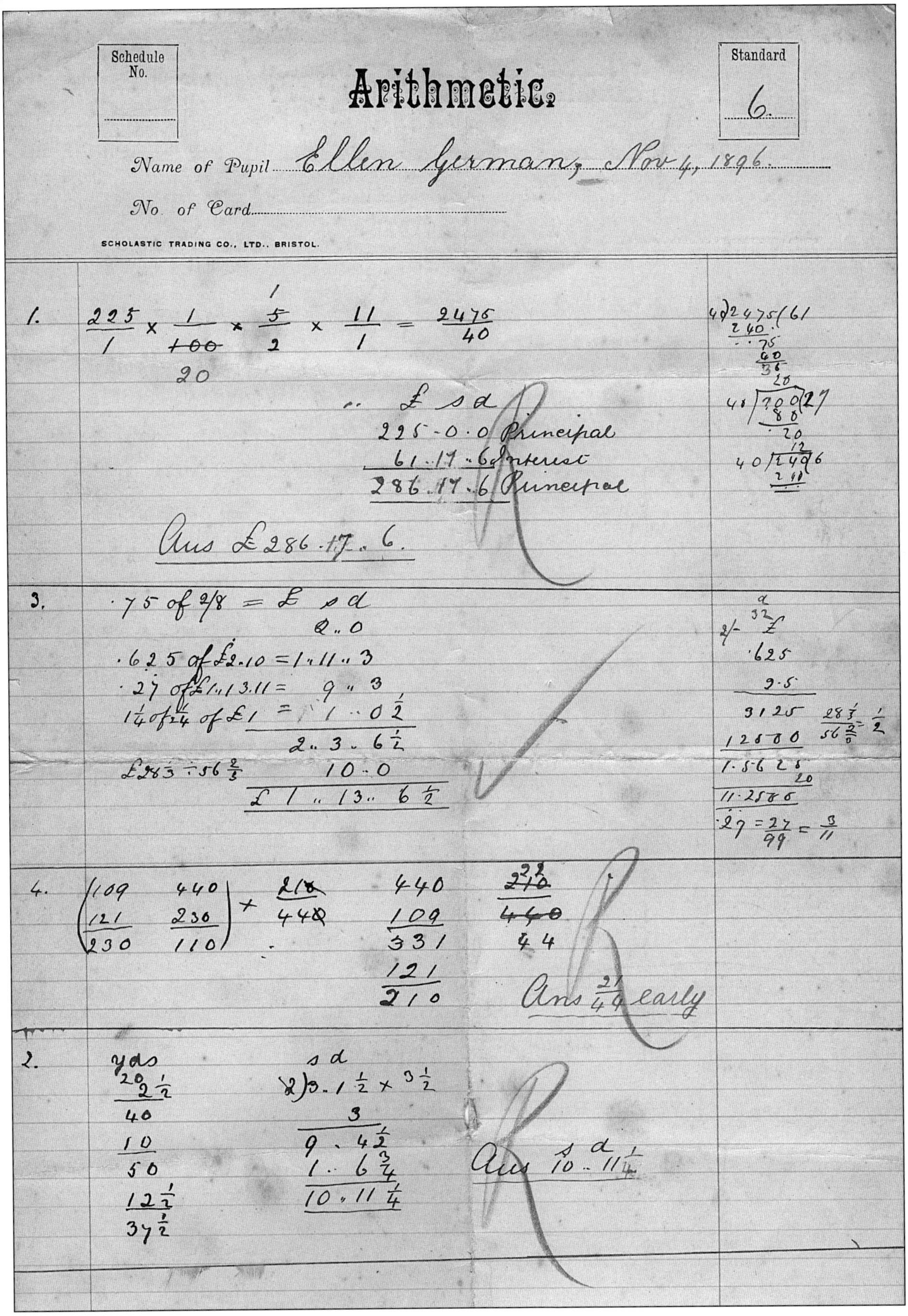

Arithmetic.

Schedule No.

Standard 6

Name of Pupil *Ellen German, Nov 4, 1896*

No. of Card

SCHOLASTIC TRADING CO., LTD., BRISTOL.

---

1. $$\frac{225}{1} \times \frac{1}{100} \times \frac{5}{2} \times \frac{11}{1} = \frac{2475}{40}$$
    20

    £ s d
    225 . 0 . 0 Principal
    61 . 17 . 6 Interest
    286 . 17 . 6 Principal

    Ans £286 . 17 . 6

    40)2475(61
    240
    75
    60
    36
    20

    40)2400(27
    80
    20
    40)2496
    211

---

3. .75 of 2/8 = £ s d
                    2 . 0
    .625 of £2.10 = 1 . 11 . 3
    .27 of £1.13.11 = 9 . 3
    1¼ of ¼ of £1 = 1 . 0 2½
                    2 . 3 . 6½
    £283 ÷ 56⅔   10 . 0
                £1 . 13 . 6½

    2/- 32
    .625
    9 . 5
    3125
    12500
    1.5625
    20
    11.2500
    .27 = 27/99 = 3/11
    28⅓ ½
    56⅔

---

4. (109 440)   210   440   210
    (121 230) + 440   109   440
    (230 110)   331   44
                          121
                          210

    Ans 21/44 nearly

---

2. yds   s d
    20   2)3 . 1½ × 3½
    2½   3
    40   9 . 4½
    10   1 . 6¾
    50   10 . 11¼
    12½
    37½

    Ans 10 . 11¼

Schoolgirl Muriel Dotson with her mother, Ellen, 1920.

large splat of potatoes and the rest are cabbages. We have had a good crop of cabbages and potatoes as it's good soil. Besides this there are gooseberry bushes by the side.

Although she notes that she has a 'little splat in the front garden' to grow some flowers, she goes on to say that:

... as we have not got a big vegetable garden we cannot grow such things as celery, lettuce or radishes. These are not of much use to us, we must grow what is the most useful. Our garden although it is small is very useful. When we want a cabbage or anything instead of buying it we can go and cut one.

Attending the school 22 years later was Ellen's daughter, who, like her mother, has left us a valuable record of her time there.

Muriel Dotson was born at Grove Cottage, St Mawes, in 1906, and was the only child of Ellen (née German) and Joe Dotson. Muriel attended the local school, and it is through her surviving school books that we are able to look back to St Mawes in the early 1900s.

What Muriel wrote in the early-twentieth century ago has left us with a wonderful picture of St Mawes in those days. From odd sentences, when she is talking about lighting the fire – 'Afterwards I light a candle and take a shovel and go to the coal house' – to the very amusing, 'I have no brothers or sisters for which I am very glad', and to her account of going by steamer to Percuil and then the walk up to Gerrans.

On 25 December 1919 she wrote:

On Christmas eve I usually go to Falmouth with my Mother or Father or sometimes with both. When I go I buy some presents for my friends. After I come home in the evening I go singing with my friends about half past six. When we have finished going to people's doors singing we share the money. Afterwards I go to my Grandmother's house with my Mother until about ten o'clock and then we go home. On Christmas day when I wake up I look into my stocking to see what is in it. After I dress I go downstairs and give my Mother and Father a present each and wish them a happy Christmas. When all that is over we have breakfast and then clear the things away and we go to my Grandmother's house. On Boxing day in the morning I generally go to Sunday School where we decorate it for the bazaar, which we have in the afternoon. At first I help to decorate the stall which some other girls and I attend to when the selling of things is on. The Bazaar is opened at three o'clock and tea is served at five. In the evening there is usually entertainment and I am often in it.

On 2 February 1920 she wrote:

I like cooking the best of any work. Because for one thing it is very useful and for another it is a thing everybody should know. I often watch my Mother making dinners and cake. Sometimes if she has a little dough left over I make a jam pasty or if she has a little meat left make a potato and meat pasty. One day when my Mother was out I made a small pasty for my tea with some dough my Mother had left. It tasted very nice, but not as good as what my Mother makes.

An entry on 9 February 1920 reads:

At this school, it is needful for us to have boxes to keep our school materials in. The desks are just a thick plank of wood and, about six inches under, there is a thinner plank to keep the school articles on. They are about twelve feet long so that four children can sit in one comfortably. My box is made of wood and is strong. In the front side of it there is a crack. I have put a pin in it to keep it together. One of the shopkeepers gave it to me for nothing. Most of the children's boxes are made of wood. I take mine home once or twice a year to scrub it.

On 3 March 1920:

The other day, I was asked about the view from our school, so I will tell you what can be seen from the window that faces the south and the one that faces the east.

Map of Italy, hand drawn by Ellen German in 1896, aged 12.

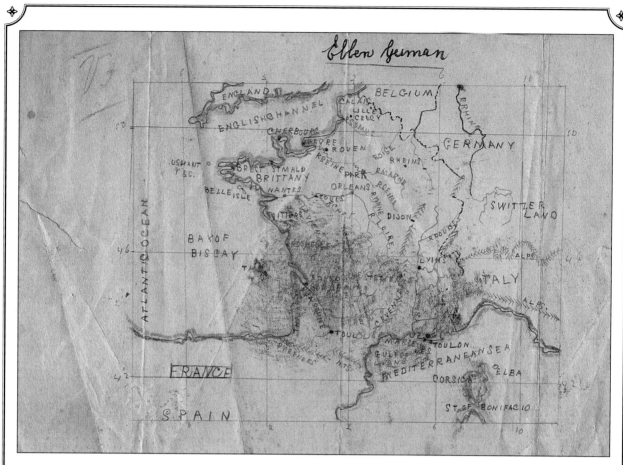

Map of France, hand drawn by Ellen German in 1896, aged 12.

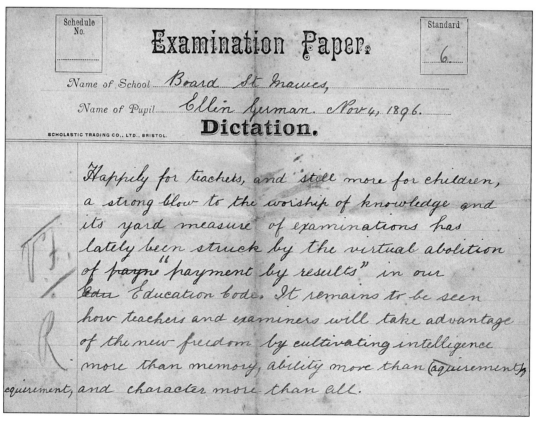

More elegant handwriting from 12-year-old Ellen German in 1896.

St Mawes school, 1914.

St Mawes school, 1918.

St Mawes infants c.1900.

St Mawes school 1931. In the middle row *are sisters Barbara, June and Megan Bryant.*

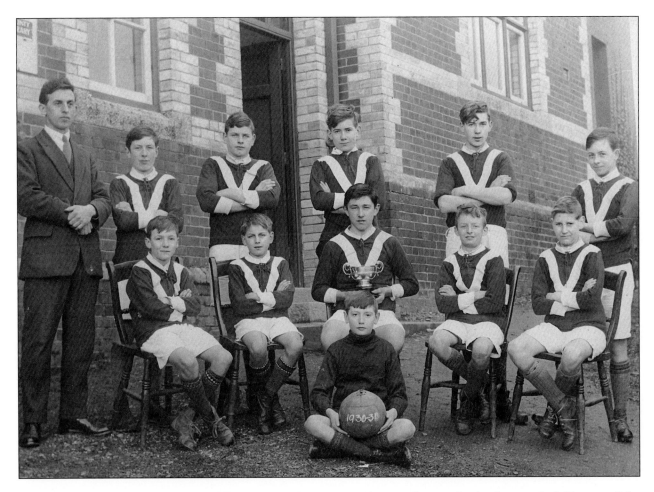

St. Mawes school football team, 1930/31, with headmaster Mr May. Left to right, back row: Jack Truscott, John German, Leslie Drinkwater, Stanley Drinkwater, Frank Sawle; front row: Fred Andrew, Jack Tiddy, Jimmy Lelean, Reg Truscott, Ken Thomas, Charlie Collins.

We can look out of this south one and see Falmouth Bay. There are no ships there now but at the commencement and during the war, quite a number were there. If you look straight in front of you, you will see St Anthony and the creek. On looking aside a little to the right, I expect you can see the coastguard station and the fort. I don't think any soldiers are there now, but a year or two ago a great many were.

The ground below the window is the boys' playground. In the distance is Trewince Wood. Looking in the opposite direction near the water, can you see that bright green grass – that is Place House.

Now, shall we go to the other window? This plot of grass belongs to the school and that is Uncle Ned's house and garden there. The Bottoms are over there; that is where we went for blackberries last year. The top row of houses is called Kennerly Terrace and those a little further down are the coastguard houses. The top one is used by the officer. That house standing in a field by itself is a farmhouse. I go there every morning for milk.

On 18 March 1920:

The Congregational Chapel stands in the front of the

town of St Mawes. There is a Sunday school at the back of it. Just opposite the gate which leads into the yard is the vestry door. On the right hand side is the door which opens into the lobby. The front of the chapel is covered with ivy. There are four tall windows with the four bottom panes frosted. The Chapel door is covered with red baize. There is only one aisle and that has coconut matting on it. Just above the door is a gallery which will hold a good many people. On each side of the Chapel are eight or nine seats, which will each hold eight persons. The walls are green washed but it is coming off now. On the right hand side there is a roll of honour and a door which leads to the wash house.

The coal, oil and pails are kept there. Opposite the Chapel door is the pulpit, and on the right hand side of that is a door which belongs to the vestry. Near it is a tablet which was erected to the memory of the Revd Gant. There are six lamps in the Chapel and one in the gallery. Each one is suspended by a chain which is fastened to the ceiling. Near the front seat on the left hand side is the harmonium.

On 25 March 1920:

About a month ago, I went for a walk with my mother

St Mawes school, c.1950.

St Mawes school, c.1950.

St Mawes School, 1959. Left to right, back row: ?, D. Collins, ?, J. Brokenshire, K. Ferris, R. Chenoweth, F. Cock, Barry Andrew, head teacher J. Collins; second row: J. Lister, ?, J. Tiddy, A. Miners, V. Juliff, G. Williams, ?; third row: Bridget Couch, C. Hooper, ? Tucker, ? Butland, Pat German, K. Clift, L. Tiddy; front row: R. Ferris, D. Clode, David Giles, ?, L. Green D. Sawle.

and father. We went to Polvarth, or at least thought we would go there. When we left home, we went up the big hill, passed the Bible Christian Chapel and into my grandma's house (Rope Walk). We stayed for a few minutes and then went on our way. After walking a few yards, we came to the brake yard and the week day school. When we had walked a little further we came to a gate and we saw two lambs and a sheep. As we walked on we came to two farmhouses. There was a yard near one with a pony in a cart in it.

A little further on we came to a signpost and then to Mrs Rundle's farm. After that we turned a corner and went down a lane with trees overhead. It was very pleasant going down that lane, also to hear the birds singing. As we went on, we came to Kennerly Terrace and there, I saw my friend, Maud Lelean, standing by her garden gate with her little brother Jim. On the opposite side of the road we sat on the seat for a while.

After we had walked a few yards, we met Mr and Mrs May and their dog Sally. A bit further on we came to a farmhouse where we saw two pretty kittens playing. Near the house was a yard where we saw three big black pigs and some cows. We went on until we came to a turning which leads to the New Road.

On 16 January 1920:

Last Saturday and Sunday we had some very bad weather here at St Mawes. On Saturday morning, I didn't go for any butter because the weather was so bad. I didn't go out much because of the rain. My mother and I were afraid to go into the yard much because the slates were coming off the roof.

About eleven o'clock, I took some lunch to my father. When I came back out from the cellar, I looked at my boots and saw that they were covered with mud that had splashed on them. On my way home, my hat blew off and I had to give chase. It blew as far as the Watch House and then it went into a pool and got wet so that I could not put it on.

On 15 April 1920:

On Wednesday, I went to Portscatho to get some meat for Thursday's dinner. By the time I was ready to go in the Steamer, the rain had stopped a little, but I took my umbrella all the same and was glad of it afterwards.

When I got on the Steamer, the rain came down again, so I went down in the cabin. I soon went up again because the throbbing of the engines made me feel sick. When I got on the deck, I opened my umbrella and went under the lifeboat. We soon reached the Steamers boat and then we didn't take long to land. When we were landed, I hurried on the road and soon came to a farmhouse and the rectory. When I reached the Gerrans clock, the hands were pointing to a quarter to twelve.

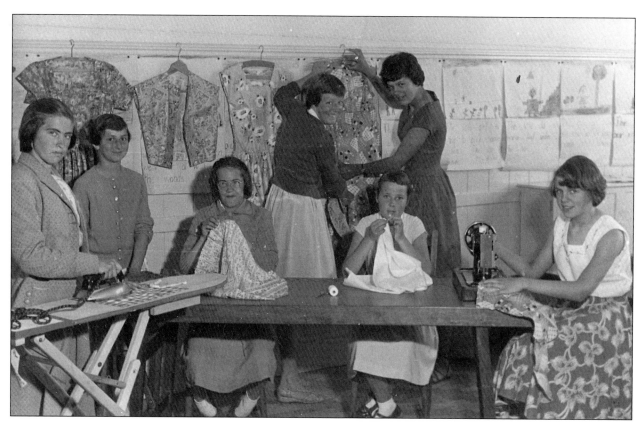

Needlework class, 1959. Bridget Gay is second from left.

On 28 October 1920:

I am a girl and my name is Muriel Ellen Dotson. I live in a four-roomed house in St Mawes with my mother and father. It is the same house that I was born in, on 20 March 1906. I have no brothers or sisters, for which I am very glad. The greatest length of time I have ever been from home is a week and that was spent at Portscatho. I have attended the Council school here since I was four years old and am now in standard seven. My friends are Louis Clode, Gladys Peters, Dora Davis and Josephine Hearn.

I learn music at Mrs Collings' and on Sundays I play in the Congregational Sunday school. My grandparents live in St Mawes and when I grow up I would like to be a schoolteacher or a milliner. When I go home from school in the winter evenings, I usually go for my mother's papers and any other errands for her. On Mondays, I go to the Band of Hope with my friend Madeline Andrew. Before tea, I have to fetch the sugar ration. During Saturday nights, I either go out with my friends, Madeline Andrew and Sylvia Dash, or go to my grandparent's house, where I read my children's newspaper.

Bathing at St Mawes is a very common and favourite enjoyment. The visitors come here and in the months of July, August and September the beach is crowded with holidaymakers. The most popular beach is Summers Beach but there is another which is nearly as well known named Tavern. All the beaches around here are

safe, there being no quicksand or swift currents. I prefer a high tide when bathing as there is not any seaweed to get tangled in. We have no bathing tents on the beach here which is rather a drawback but there are several caves which are used instead. Some people fix up their own tents each day. Most people around here can swim but I cannot. My friends are teaching me.

On 27 July 1921:

Last Saturday we had a picnic. We had all the baskets packed and were on the quay waiting for my Father to come for us in the boat by three o'clock. We went up the river to Percuil and then we waited a while as we were expecting my aunts and three cousins to join us there. After five minutes of waiting we saw them come around the corner with a pushchair and baskets. When they had all got into the boat, we pulled up to Tuckers Beach and landed. We played stones and just when it was getting to an interesting point my Father said it was time to go home.

On 27 October 1921:

The annual vegetable and poultry show was held at St Mawes on Monday week. In the United Methodist Sunday School the birds were shown and the council School was used for the fruit and vegetables. To enter the fee was sixpence, and you would have a ticket given you which would admit you to the other room as well. Some of the fowls in the Sunday School were very fine also there was a large show of canaries. On the platform at the front were the rabbits and at the back were a number of cats some of which were very frightened, and next to them were pigeons and bantams. Vegetables were on show in the largest room of the Council School and a big number of flowers which were very beautiful. There were parsnips, carrots and potatoes which were an enormous size. For the enterer who had the highest numbers in the fruit section there was a silver plated butter dish. I have heard since that it was the best show held at St Mawes for many years.

On 8 December 1921:

With the Cornish miners there has been for the last year, and is now, great distress. The price of tin has fallen and there has not been the sale for it, so consequently the men have been out of work. Four choirs have been organized at Redruth and Cambourne to sing at different places and collect money which is equally distributed among those in distress. On Sunday November 27 one of the choirs came to St Mawes to give two sacred concerts in the Wesleyan Church. They came from Redruth in a char-a-banc and reached here at a quarter past one. They were met on the top of the hill by members of the four different Churches and taken to private houses to dinner. There were 36 men, so nine were distributed to each Church. We had one man of the name of Tresidder and from whom we learned that the choir was one that had been organized about 20 years

ago, and had competed with Falmouth Male Voice Choir for the Championship of Cornwall this year. After Xmas they are going to London to sing before the King for charity. The afternoon commenced at three o'clock, so at half past two my Father went with Mr Tresidder and a few minutes afterwards my uncle and I went. The concert was a great success, both scared and sentimental songs were given. A Mr Uglow addressed the congregation on the distress at Camborne and Redruth and how the money was being spent. At half past four the concert came to a close. The evening concert was also a success. Supper was provided for the miners before they left for home.

In 1918 a local newspaper reported that:

A remarkable record has been set up by little Muriel Dotson, daughter of Mr and Mrs Joe Dotson, Grove Cottage. Aged 12 years, she has attended school for the past six and a half years, not once being either absent or late. On hearing of this creditable record, Sir George Smith awarded Muriel a bound volume of the Girl's Own Annual, *and unable to be present through indisposition, he delegated Mr Spargo James to make the presentation, which took place recently. Inside the front cover is inscribed: 'Presented to Muriel Dotson by Sir George Smith, chairman of the District Education Committee, in recognition of her six and a half years of punctual and unbroken attendance at St Mawes Council School.'*

The Victory Inn in 1889, at that time kept by J.A. Dotson. Beer was brewed at the back of the pub.

✦ CHAPTER 13 ✦

The Old Inns

It is not too surprising that the old inns of St Mawes were all grouped around the harbour, as this is where the majority of the trade was to be found. The coming and going of sailors, the crews of the many cargo boats that unloaded on the quay and the passengers who were waiting to board the ships which lay at anchor in the bay, all went to make this a very busy harbour.

In April 1814 a dinner was held at the Lord Nelson Inn at St Mawes to celebrate the final defeat of Napoleon. The inn had existed under that name since 1804.

On the quay stood the long-established St Mawes Arms. A survey was held there in 1780, and the inn, which was often used by foreign sailors, was the scene of several public order offences.

Rather an unexpected name to find in St Mawes was that of the Hamburg Arms. The town in those

The Victory Inn, a photograph taken in the 1960s.

The old Rising Sun, 1890.

days held strong ties with Hamburg – in 1765 Hamburg and Bremen ordered several thousand barrels of pilchards from the Falmouth merchant Joseph Banfield. Much of this order was purchased at St Mawes, the catch being transported aboard the Danish brig *Anna Margarita*. There was also a ship called the *Hamburg*, from Bordeaux, a frequent visitor around these shores, which was wrecked fully laden off the Lizard in 1769.

St Mawes also boasted the Shipwright's Arms, which was run in 1841 by Joseph Hancock. In that same year John Hancock took over as landlord of the Old Rising Sun from Jane Hancock, who was recorded as the licensee in 1873. By 1914 William Frederick Clode was holding the licence. The still-flourishing Victory Inn, built in 1841 originally as a house, was run by the Dotson family and they, like most of the other landlords at that time, brewed their own ale on the premises. There was, however, a malt house in Lower Castle Road and another at Chapel Terrace. John Whiston was a maltster living and working in St Mawes in 1814.

Mrs Sarah Dotson held the licence of the Victory in 1873 and continued as landlady until 1889, when the licensee is recorded as John Arthur Dotson. The census of 1914 lists James Liddy as the landlord.

In 1873 the New Inn was kept by Alfred Bellman. Other historic inns at St Mawes included the Fountain Inn, which in 1873 was being run by Mrs Jane Rickard. By 1884 it was in the care of James Lean. The previous year the licence was in the hands of Mr William Kendall, who also held the licence of the Commercial Inn and the Queen's Head, which was situated just around the corner and up the hill from the Watch House. Back in 1873 Joseph Lower held the licence at the Queen's Head .

The Fountain eventually became the St Mawes Hotel and the licence passed to William Rickard, who was the proprietor in 1883, having taken over from Mrs Mary Belman. By 1914 the licensee was Harry May. In 1884 the Queen's Head was run by Charles Green.

In the reign of Elizabeth I, it is recorded in the Powder hundred list that the innkeepers of St Mawes were:

Xth daie of September in the XlXth yere of the relgn of our Soveraigne Ladie Elizabeth the Queens majestie. The parish of St Just and the village of St Mawys. John Hore, Henry Ball, Stephen Higo, Innkeepers.

Halfway between St Mawes and St Just, on the cliff above St Just creek, stood the White House Inn. This Inn was well sited to serve the needs of the many ships that anchored in the shelter of the river in the 1700s. In St Just itself, you could be well accommo-

The old Rising Sun, run by Jane Hancock.

Jane Hancock, landlady of the Rising Sun, c.1900.

dated at the Seven Stars, which was run for 100 years by the Tiddy family, being in the tender care of Mr John Tiddy in 1831.

Also at St Just was the Ship Inn, which was run by the Wakeham family. They had held the licence from the early 1700s to 1876, when the former landlord of the Plume of Feathers at Portscatho, Mr Bosustow, took it over. The inn was the scene of two fires. It survived the first in 1886, but four years later was completely gutted.

And so there were a good number of inns for a small seaside town, though the population in 1871 was calculated at 1,000. If you also consider the passing trade, sailors coming and going, etc., the waterfront must have been a hive of activity.

Left: *The Victory Inn in the 1940s, when the licensee was W.T. Hodge.*

Below: *George Bryant* (bottom left) *enjoying a pint at the Rising Sun in the early 1960s.*

CHAPTER 14

A New Life

In the 1800s several St Mawes-based families, like many others in Cornwall, decided to look for pastures new. The thought of a new life with higher wages must have held great appeal. One such family were the Vercoes.

Philip Vercoe was born in St Austell in 1775. In 1801 he married Jane Odgers of St Anthony in Roseland. Philip was working as a stonemason at this time. They moved to St Mawes and it was there that their seven children were born. By 1814 they

Thomas Dotson, c.1880.

Sam Dotson, who worked as a carpenter in South Africa and Canada before returning to St Mawes.

Sam Dotson and two work mates. All of them worked for Edwin Hicks.

were leasing a cottage in St Austell Row. Of Phillip and Jane's seven children, four emigrated to New Zealand and one to Austraila. Their son Samuel died at the age of 23 and was buried at St Just churchyard. Only their daughter, Mary, continued to live in St Mawes, where she married John Vincent.

John Vercoe was the first of the family to leave. He and his wife Peggy arrived in Sydney aboard the *James Pettimam* in September 1838. Their two children, Samuel, aged two, and a baby born on the voyage, both died on the trip. Although John was a stonemason like his father, he opened a Temperance coffee shop in Pitt Street, Sydney, between 1841 and 1843. Times were very hard for him and his family and so they sailed to New Zealand on the *Tryphena* in 1843. Unfortunately John did not live to enjoy New Zealand, and died in November of that year.

The other four children left St Mawes and travelled directly to New Zealand – Jane with her husband John Hooker, Phillip with his wife Catherine Collins and their nine children, Bryant

with his wife Elizabeth Tiddy and their two children and the unmarried Martha Vercoe. They all travelled aboard the *Timandra*, a 382-ton barque which sailed from Plymouth on 2 November 1841, arriving at New Plymouth on 23 February 1842. Most of the 212 emigrants were from Devon and Cornwall. And so that movement of the Vercoe family accounted for a loss of 22 persons from St Mawes.

Reading the ship's log reveals that the reality of a long sea voyage in those days was something not to be taken lightly. Five children died, one of them James Vercoe, the two-year-old son of Bryant and Elizabeth, and one adult also died. Of the two children born on board, one died at only three weeks old. According to the log the 'General character of the emigrants was disappointing, temper, swearing, filth and theft from the steerage passengers being rampant.' The ship carried two classes of emigrant, those who had purchased land and those 'travelling on the Parish'. When the ship's doctor asked for volunteers to assist in keeping order, one Mr Vercoe put himself forward. Whether this was Phillip or Bryant is unclear, but they were given the power to act as constables to enforce regulations. For this they were promised a reward within the doctor's power to give, although what this reward may have been is not recorded. Not all the emigrants were badly behaved, as the Vercoes, Brookings, Harrisons, Allans, Treweitts, Clares and Prousts were said to be good emigrants for the colony.

Mary Vercoe, who stayed in St Mawes, married

Sam and Annie Dotson photographed in Canada, c.1930.

Sam and Annie's son, Cyril, was born in Canada.

John Vincent, a shoemaker, on 17 August 1814 and they had several children – Martha, Samuel, Nicholas, John and, finally, Philip. Mary, who did not recover after the birth of her last child, died soon afterwards.

In 1906 a young carpenter, Richard German, decided to follow in the footsteps of those who had gone before, and headed out west. Richard settled in Philadelphia and wrote home regularly to his married sister, Ellen Dotson. On 30 November 1907 he wrote, 'Received your postcard, glad you are all well. I'm ok, working. Too busy to write letters. Love to all from Richard.' Although Richard never returned to St Mawes, he did marry however and had a daughter.

Another travelling carpenter from St Mawes was Sam Dotson. Samuel Dotson was born in St Mawes in 1865, the son of local fisherman Thomas Dotson. Sam first went to South Africa in the late 1800s and later recalled being taken ashore in a basket, as docks or proper berths had yet to be built. After a while he

decided to return to St Mawes, where he worked for Edwin Hicks. Edwin had also worked in South Africa for some time. After marrying local girl Annie Vincent, the couple decided to try their luck in Canada. In 1910 he wrote home from Avonmouth Dock in Bristol to his brother Joe: 'Just leaving docks, everything is splendid. Annie and I have cabin to ourselves.' Annie and Sam had a son, Cyril, who was born and who died in Canada. Sam and Annie returned to St Mawes when Annie's health failed. Sam spent the rest of his life working around the village at his trade. His tools and the tool chest which accompanied him on his travels are still intact.

When Sam's father died in 1899

Left: *Richard German, carpenter of St Mawes, settled in Philadelphia.*

The Rope Walk in the 1920s.

Pomery's charabanc, c.1930. The passengers include a young Donald Pollard with his aunt Ellen Dotson. The driver is possibly Will Andrews.

The whole village turned out to celebrate the 1936 coronation of Edward VIII.

St Mawes during the 1936 celebrations of the coronation of Edward VIII.

Top and above: *Ned Dotson leading the Coronation carnival, 1936.*

he named his executors as William Collins Dotson, Samuel Arthur Lowry Dotson and Joseph James Dotson, his sons. In his Will he gave Joseph 'for his own use all my share and interest in the boats and gear used by me and my son in connection with our business as fishermen, and I also give and bequeath unto my said son Joseph for his own use and benefit all the household furniture and effects in my dwelling house at St Mawes.' He left all the rest of his personal property to his two other sons and his daughter, Agnes Gertrude Hyde Dotson. What exactly was left to share after Joseph had been bequeathed the boats, the gear and household affects

is not clear, but the value of his estate was £328.14s.3d., a good deal of money in 1899.

St Mawes Policeman Assaulted

On 23 June 1920, a report was published in the *Falmouth Packet* with the headline 'Excitement at St Mawes':

Police Constable Tonkin of St Mawes and four poachers had a lively encounter in the village in the early hours of Sunday morning. In the course of several interviews with residents in the usually peaceful and law abiding

Top and above: *The Coronation carnival, 1936.*

The 1936 coronation tea, held at the school.

village this week, our representative was informed that for some considerable period, a great deal of poaching had been in progress in the locality. Suspicion rested on four young men, only two of whom reside at St Mawes.

Between three and four a.m. on Sunday, several of the inhabitants were greatly frightened to hear the noise of a scuffle and cries for assistance and on several running into the road (some in their night attire) it was found that PC Tonkin had been severely handled and was lying on the ground incapable of action. Indeed it is understood that, had it not been for the prompt help of an innkeeper, who obtained restoratives, the result would have been most serious.

It appears that the constable was on duty near the Rising Sun Inn, when he saw the four men approaching. One was carrying a gun and another, a bag. He stopped them and demanded the gun and bag and, upon discovering the contents of the latter, asked the offenders to accompany him. They then attacked him, with the result that the unfortunate officer was very roughly handled. The men made off and the officer

was unable to follow them owing to his exhausted condition. They were identified and will be prosecuted for assault.

St Mawes Coronation Celebrations

The account books for the St Mawes celebrations in 1936 of the coronation of King Edward VIII give a good picture of village life at that time, gifts for the occasion including 34lbs of beef and four gallons of milk, given by Mr J. Hancock, 6lbs of butter from Miss Pasco of Trethem and the loan of a lorry from Mr J. Michell.

The children of the parish were to receive 192 spoons and 180 boxes of chocolates, which were to be presented by Lady Arran. The Salvation Army band had been booked to play on the quay for a fee of £10.10s. Cars were hired for the day from Mr Jack Green and Mr Chester. At that time 1cwt of coal was just 2s.4d. and the cost of teas provided for the 'sick and aged' amounted to £16.6s.8d.

A coal boat at St Mawes, c.1930.

In 1929 coal was still being delivered to St Mawes by boat.

Memories

Charlie Collins

Mother and Sheba would come down to St Mawes from Plymouth on the day before Christmas Eve. They would catch the 13.30 train from Keyham Station. This stopped at all the stations to Truro, where they transferred to the local train for Falmouth, which arrived at 16.30. This gave them time to walk down from Penmere Halt, and catch the 17.30 steamer from the Prince of Wales pier. Father had to work on Christmas Eve morning and would catch the Cornish Rivera Express from North Road Station.

I remember one Xmas Eve there was a terrific gale blowing and it was low tide when the last steamer arrived at St Mawes and moored at the buoy off the quay. Charles Dash and someone else managed to row the large rowing boat out to the steamer and the passengers got in, though Father did not. On the way into the quay one huge wave lifted the boat and carried it in towards the rocks below the Idle Rocks Hotel. The rowers, there were four of them now, somehow kept the boat upright and it made the quay. I had gone to meet Father and was standing on the end of the quay and saw this happen. They did not attempt to land any more passengers by boat. The steamer went to a mooring at St Anthony and Father landed there.

On Christmas Eve children formed groups of five or six and went carol singing. The boys blackened

The German family in 1909. Left to right, back row: Rose German, Richard German, Ellen German; front row: Emma German, Richard Jane German, Annie German, Ellen Alma German, Fleetwood German.

their faces with burnt cork and carried hollowed out mangles with a lighted candle inside. The singing was at least three or four complete carols and we made a point of concentrating on the church- and chapel-going people, expecting about sixpence to be given by them. At the end of the evening we shared the takings which were in the order of 2s. (10p) each.

Left to right: *John Andain, Mary Jago Pasco, Hubert and John Andain (sitting with his father).*

During the 1920s and 1930s most of the large houses in St Mawes were unoccupied, as this was the era of the slump. One of those occupied was Harding's, the thatched house on the point at the entrance to Percuil River. We would sing there and usually received mince pies, but no money.

On one Christmas Eve I was over at Aunt Rose Sawle, Douglas' mother, and she wanted something from Andain's shop. Douglas and I went for it, and ran down the back road. It was pitch dark, not a light showing anywhere, and it was raining. As we ran around the corner at the back of the St Mawes Hotel, we bumped into someone. We ran on and went into the shop, and then returned to Aunt Rose's. A little while later the next door neighbour came in, Miss Moyle, she was only about four foot 6 inches tall and she was complaining that she had been knocked down, her umbrella broken and her dress made dirty. We brushed her down not letting on it was us.

Preparations for Christmas started during the summer, when eggs were pickled in large brown earthenware jars of isinglass. The eggs were then used in Christmas cakes. The cakes were made at the beginning of November and it was always a major operation. One of my tasks was to sit at the table and sift through the currants, raisins and sultanas, making sure that all the pips were removed.

The cake mixing was done in a large earthenware bowl and we all had to take turns at stirring. The mixture was then placed in the cake tins, the largest being about 10 inches in diameter.

The cakes, about two at a time, were placed in the oven of the coal stove. These were moments of great

Cyril Green enjoying a quiet moment at St Mawes Harbour in 1930.

A sailors' haven in the 1930s.

tension while the cakes were cooking, in case they did not rise. When they were deemed to be ready all the doors to the room were closed and were not allowed to be opened in case a draught made the cakes collapse. Then they were taken out and placed on the kitchen table to cool.

This operation took place several times, as up to 10 cakes were made.

A few weeks before Christmas the icing of some of the cakes was done on the dining-room table, usually by Dain.

Christmas pudding making, like cakes, was again a major operation, with many being made several weeks before Christmas. They were boiled in a large cast-iron container on the stove. The pudding mixture was placed in a white basin and covered by a white linen cloth, tied in a knot at the top. By this it was lifted in and out of the pot.

Ox tongue was another preparation for Christmas. It was boiled in a large cast-iron container on the stove. When cooked it was taken out and placed in a round press. The top was put on and screwed down, compressing the tongue. This was eaten at supper over the Christmas period.

Ham was also cooked and served for supper.

Pickling onions was also a part of the Christmas catalogue. This started at the end of August, when shallots were bought. During the evening they were peeled and put into large jars with vinegar and cloves.

In the garden was a Bramley apple tree, from which there was always a large crop of really big apples. These were picked and placed on shelves in the dark cupboard under the stairs. They were then used as required throughout the winter, usually with apple pie and cream. There was always a large apple pie for Christmas.

The turkey (we always had turkey) arrived from one of the local farms three or four days before Christmas. It was complete with head, feathers, insides and feet. The feathers had to be plucked, which was quite a long job, especially picking out the small ends of quills that remained. The turkey was then scorched with a lighted candle to burn off all the ends that remained. After cleaning and washing it was placed in the outside safe until Christmas morning.

Auntie Sheba (Sawle) made a sponge for every Sunday tea (made from 'green' sponge mixture unkown today). For Christmas she made at least two, and these were eaten at tea time on Christmas Day and Boxing Day, with large spoonfuls of cream.

Drinks such as beer, spirits and such like were never around. There was usually a bottle of sherry received as a present, but this was put away in the cupboard and used sparingly over the next year.

We had plenty of mixed nuts placed on the table to help ourselves. Using the nutcracker when we were small restricted the amount we could eat.

There was very little drinking at all in homes over Christmas or at any other time. Uncle Harold Watts made sloe wine and Uncle Alf Pascoe (Granny Sawle and Uncle Fred's brother) made several kinds of home-made wine. Men went to the four public

Muriel Dotson and Maud Lelean, 1926.

Katie Hawkin, Mr Alfred Pasco's daughter c.1930.

houses, the Rising Sun, the Victory Inn, the Ship & Castle and the St Mawes Hotel, and over Christmas and New Year quite a lot of noise and singing came from here. Ladies did not go into public houses in those days.

Going to bed on Christmas Eve, I always hung my pillowcase at the bottom of the bed. The next day it contained oranges, apples, a coconut, sweets and maybe one toy, and when I was a little older mother's present was a dictionary or an atlas.

It was all hustle and bustle on Christmas morning, with Aunt Sheba, my mother and father and sister Sheba, with Douglas and myself sitting in the window seat.

Christmas tea was in the lower front room. During the afternoon Dain would arrive and he would play games with us. Tea was Christmas cake, tinned fruit, mince pies, sponge, tartlets and cream scones. We had cream with everything.

The coal fire was topped up with logs and the room was warm. In the evening we played games – Ludo, and Snakes and Ladders.

There were a few decorations put up in the front room. The main item was a real tree, and this was placed in a large container of earth. The glass decorations were similar to those we get now, but the lights were small candles placed in small tin candle holders to catch the grease. The candles had to be watched very carefully so that they did not catch the tree on fire.

Auntie Louie Watts – Ena, Jack and Dixie's mother and my mother's sister – held a Christmas party for the family children at her house, Malcom Villa. This house was named after the last ship Uncle Harold served on in the Royal Navy. He was an engineer lieutenant.

Those going to the party would be myself and Sheba, Frank, Douglas, Sheba and Charlie Sawle, their father Frank, Mary Pascoe, Kathleen Vincent and Phyllis and Kathleen Sawle.

One year the owner of the Ship & Castle Hotel, an American, gave a Christmas party for the children of St Mawes. This was held in the large room over the bar, and hotel staff served the tea. Afterwards games were played and Father Christmas gave each child a present. I cannot remember any kind of celebration at all for New Year's Eve.

Presents were not distributed among families as they are now. Each mother and father gave presents to their own children but not to brothers, sisters or cousins or friends. They just did not have money to do it even if they wanted to.

The average working man's wage in the late 1920s and 1930s was £2 or £3 a week.

A Women's Institute garden party, 1939.

During the 1920s we had no electricity or running water. Cooking was on a coal apparatus on one side of the dining-room. The apparatus, as it was called, was cleaned every day with brushes and black lead. The fire was raked out and ashes taken out to a pile in the garden.

One of my jobs was to saw up and chop firewood down in the backhouse. I got short wood offcuts from Edwin Hicks' workshop down the hill. When the old Rising Sun and the surrounding houses were pulled down I carried long beams and old wood up to the backhouse, which became three-quarters full.

Permanently on the apparatus was a large black cast-iron kettle, and this was the main source of hot water.

The fire was lit early in the morning and kept alight until late at night. On Saturday evenings in the winter I was bathed in front of the fire in a galvanised bath, with water from the large kettle.

Another of my jobs was to keep the coal bucket full. This was required twice a day, a large stack of coal being kept in the backhouse. Flat irons for ironing clothes were heated on top of the apparatus.

There was always a shortage of water in St Mawes, and during the summer it was cut off from the main supply for most of the day.'

Uncle Harold Watts was the water engineer, and he had a thankless job in trying to supply any water at all. The big white tank at Waterloo was built in about 1930, with a windmill to pump the water up to it from springs at Freshwater. Uncle Harold put mains water into Auntie Sheba's in 1930. Prior to that all water had to be fetched and stored in buckets.

Rainwater was stored in large water barrels, one outside the top backhouse, three very large ones outside the back door and kitchen, and one at the bottom garden for flushing the lavatory, which was situated down there.

The large barrels were, I think, those that had in previous years been used for salting away the pilchards that were then caught at St Mawes.

Another of my jobs was keeping the water buckets full. This meant fetching water from the tap in the back lane when water was available, or going down the hill at the back of Manor House to the well. Here there was a pump with a large iron handle which brought water up from the well alongside. This water was used for drinking and cooking. The water in the barrels outside was used for washing and things like that. There being no electricity, lighting at night was by paraffin lamps and candles. The glass chimneys became black with smeech and these had to be cleaned regularly. The wicks of the lamps also had to be trimmed.

All the shops in St Mawes sold paraffin. We had a two-gallon can which I used to carry from the shops. We did finally have a five-gallon drum in the backhouse which I had to keep topped up.

There was no street lighting in the village until just before the war, probably 1937. We found our way around with flashlights, as they were called then.

The fires in the two front rooms were coal and logs. We also had a primus, which was used for boiling water. It was heated by methylated spirit and, when hot, was pumped up to burn paraffin.

The mail came from Falmouth on the 9.15a.m. steamer and was taken to the Post Office.

The St Mawes delivery was done by Mr Griffiths. He lived in the house on Big Hill and was also the town crier. The outlying district, St Just and all the surrounding farms were covered by Oswald Dash, who had a horse and wagonette.

A group of local ladies enjoying an afternoon on the beach in the 1940s. Muriel Dotson is dressed in white.

Outgoing mail had to be posted at the Post Office and went to Falmouth on the 4.15p.m. steamer. Oswald Dash always arrived from his rounds at the brake yard next to the school at 4.00pm. He was usually loaded with sacks of mail and loose parcels. The boys coming out of school took the parcels and ran down to the Post Office, where they were thrown quickly into sacks and taken down to the steamer.

The town crier had a bell, which he rang and then announced some event that was taking place, e.g. a whist drive, a concert or a dance and, during the summer, the times water would be on and off.

In St Mawes there were four grocers' shops. On the front were H.S. Edmonds, Andain Bros and Cocks, and around the back of the Victory Inn was H. Dash.

These shops were supplemented by twice-weekly visits from Truro of vans which toured the villages. They were Maypole and Home & Colonial.

There was one butcher's shop, just off the quay. This was owned by Mr Rundle until 1933, when John Hancock of Newton Farm, brought it. Tommy Drinkwater, who was later a Spitfire fighter pilot, was the butcher. He killed the cattle in the slaughterhouse above the castle, watched by many children.

There was a combined ironmonger's and haberdashery shop, owned by Edmonds but run by Tom Jennings.

Alongside the shop was the old Post Office. This was the last commercial place up towards the castle.

If a telegram arrived for delivery a red flag was placed outside the Post Office door. Boys kept watch for the flag and when it appeared there was a race. The boy who took the flag down delivered the telegram and, on return to the Post Office, received a penny.

The chemist was J.H. Andain, which was part of Andain Bros, the grocers.

Along the front was Pomeroy's Garage. The petrol sold was Shellmex, BP, National Benzol and Pratts. Every Wednesday and Friday, Harry Andrew drove the charabanc to Truro. It was a solid-wheel open carriage and if it rained they pulled up the canvas top.

The next building was the coal store. Joe Dotson was the coalman and he delivered the coal all over St Mawes with his horse and cart. One morning going to school we found the horse dropped dead going up Big Hill.

Daily newspapers were bought from the grocers' shops, the biggest supplier being Andain Bros.

Until 1926 the daily papers arrived at St Mawes on the 3.15p.m. steamer from Falmouth. These were then delivered by the paper boys when they came out of school at 4p.m.

Around 1926 this changed and the papers arrived on the 11a.m. steamer and were delivered by the boys at lunchtime. The Andain paper-boys were Douglas Cropper, who delivered from the shop to the castle, Jack Tiddy, from the shop up Big Hill to the school,

Douglas Sawle did the back streets and I did the Hotels and Bohilla. Our wages were 2s.6d. a week and a bag of sweets.

The Sunday newspapers came to Mrs Ferris, at the house on the front. The sea wall in front of her house became the focal place for men and boys discussing football.

None of the shops sold bread until the small shop on the quay opened in about 1930, selling bread from a Gerrans bakery. There was a bakery for a while behind the Wesleyan chapel. This was a very old bakery but it kept opening and closing down. We obtained our bread from a Falmouth baker called Trewin. He came over every day in a small motor-boat with three large wicker baskets of bread. These were placed on a trolley, which he and his son pushed around the village. He arrived at about 12p.m. and left about 4p.m. It was only on rare occasions that the weather was too rough for him, and when it was he came by van via the King Harry Ferry. There was also a baker's van that came from a Gerrans bakery called Quintrell's.

Milk was not sold in the shops. This came from Willy Mitchell from Waterloo farm, John Mitchell from Polvarth farm and John Hancock at Newton farm. Willy Mitchell came around in the mornings, helped by his sister, Lena Edwards. Jack Truscott also did a round with his horse and cart, in the morn-

ings and the evenings. He left the milk at the Post Office, and anyone who wanted milk had to knock at the side door.

I used to get our evening milk from Polvarth Farm. I had a pint can to carry the milk. Often I went out into the fields and brought the cows in to the milking shed and the can was filled up direct from the cow.

When electricity came to St Mawes, Waterloo Farm installed a separator and made separated cream, which is what they now call double cream.

At Polvarth Farm they carried on making clotted cream by warming large pans of milk on a stove and then putting them into a cold dairy. This was done by Ruby Mitchell, Pat Sawle's mother.

Butter and eggs were not sold in the shops, and these had to be obtained from the farms. Leyland Mitchell farmed at Tredellans, past St Just. He came into St Mawes on Saturday evenings selling butter, the proceeds being spent in the pubs. He had a horse and trap and the horse knew its own way home. Auntie Sheba had some butter from Leyland and the remainder, including eggs, I used to get from Waterloo Farm, first when farmed by Rundles and then by Willy Mitchell.

Only small quantities of butter and milk were kept at a time, especially in the summer, because in those days there were no refrigerators. Butter, cream,

The staff of Edmonds' shop in the 1950s. From left to right: *Linda from Falmouth, Muriel Dotson, George Davis, ?, Brenda Brokenshaw.*

The staff at Edmonds' shop in 1958. The girls are Yvonne Kittow and Muriel Dotson.

The interior of Edmonds' shop.

May Couch and Muriel Dotson standing outside Edmonds' shop c.1930. Muriel worked in the Edmonds family shop all her working life.

milk and meat were kept in a safe, which was attached to the wall outside the back door. It was like a small cupboard with a perforated galvanised door.

Eggs could not be obtained in the winter. I do not know why. Towards the end of the summer eggs were pickled in very large stone jars.

Shoe repairs were done by Melville Chester in the small shop below Manor House. He also had an Austin 12 car, which at that time was the only taxi that could be hired, except for the one from Pomeroy's Garage. He was hired twice a week for many years to take Auntie Mabel to Truro for treatment for arthritis. We also used him to go to St Austell to catch the train.

When the Americans arrived in the area Mr

Chester got the contract for repairing their boots. He worked day and night, made a lot of money and eventually bought up most of the shops and a lot of property.

There were two fishermen, Willy Green and Jack Ferris. They returned about 4 or 5 o'clock and one of their sons carried the fish around the village from door to door. The fish sold at about 1d. or 2d each, depending on the size.

Around 1930 the shop on the quay opened. It sold bread but during the summer sold ice-cream. Vera and Flora Sawle, my cousins, ran this shop.

Prior to this the only ice-cream you could get was from Bob Borlace, who came down from St Just in his horse and trap. He went up and down the front from the castle to the end of New Road. I was forbidden by Aunt Sheba to buy from him because he was not supposed to be clean. But he did sell halfpenny cornets, and the ice-cream was very good. All the children bought one when they had some money.

A barber came once a week and used a ramshackle place over Hicks' store just off the quay. He would catch the steamer from Falmouth. This meant having a haircut during the dinner time from school. He would make boys wait if any men came in and sometimes we had to go without getting cut so that we could get back to school. Most times I went up to White City to Ernie Whitford, who cut hair in the kitchen for 3d.

There were two doctors in St Mawes, Dr Murray and Dr Wallace. They both lived at the top of Church Hill. Dr. Wallace was my doctor and attended me when I broke my arm. He owned an open-seater MG Midget. For some unknown reason he crashed going down the hill into St Just and was killed.

There was no dentist in the village and I can't remember anyone seeing a dentist. I suppose that they had to go to Falmouth.

Until the early 1930s there was no bank in St Mawes. A man from Lloyds Bank in Falmouth came over twice a week and used a room over the St Mawes steamship office.

An annual event was the two days of racing for the J class yachts. These were the largest yachts built. The starting line was on a line from St Anthony Lighthouse and they raced out around a marker off the Manacles, then up-channel to another marker and into the lighthouse.

The triangular course was covered twice and the yachts were in sight for the whole race. The race started at 10a.m. and would end about 4p.m. or 6p.m., depending on the wind.

The four yachts began to assemble in Falmouth several days before the event. They sailed to Falmouth bay, then dropped their sails and were towed to moorings opposite the docks. St Mawes and Pendennis Castles were crowded with sightseers to view the yachts as they were towed in. There were exceptional crowds for the arrival of the *Shamrock IV*

Stormy weather as men try to secure the boats in 1956.

St Mawes from Castle Hill in 1956.

A young Keith Ferris helping his Granddad in the garden in 1952.

& V and the *Endeavour I & II* because these yachts were to go over to America and challenge for the Americas Cup. They did not win. Thomas Lipton owned the *Shamrock* and Tom Sopwith owned the *Endeavour*.

There was a school holiday for the two days the races were held and few went to work.

I went with Uncle Frank Sawle and Douglas in their boat over to Place House and then walked out to the cliffs by St Anthony lighthouse. From there we had a perfect view of the whole course. These cliffs were crowded with people.

The yachts taking part were the *Britannia* (painted black), the *Westward II* (a two-masted schooner), the *Shamrock IV & V* (painted green), the *Endeavour I & II* (painted pale blue) the *Astrid*, the *Candida*, the *Cambria*, the *White Heather*, the *Vlhada*, the *Germania* and the *Enterprise*.

Sunday-school tea parties were held in the summer for the three chapels: Congregational, Wesleyan and the Bible Christians.

The events were held in the top field of John Hancock's farm at Newton. A silver band was in attendance and played while the sports and the tea took place. The opening part was the sports events: running and three-legged races, following which the schoolchildren of the appropriate chapel sat down at long trestle tables to their tea. This comprised a large saffron bun, jelly and tea.

In the evening everyone marched down to the quay behind the band and boarded the steamer *St Mawes*. The steamer was always packed as people,

Arial view of the village in 1957.

Three generations of the Collins family. Joseph (granddad) Michael Charles (baby), William Charles and Marilyn (granddaughter). Marion Collins stands on the left.

irrespective of the chapel, went for a trip. The band played and the trip was around St Mawes Castle up to St Just and around the old training ship *Implacable* into the docks, passing the *Fuedroyant* and the *Cutty Sark*, turning, and out to the lighthouse and then back to St Mawes. The *Fuedroyant* and the *Implacable* were old wooden Naval vessels, like the *Victory*.

We did this three times, once for each of the chapels, separated by about two weeks.

St Mawes Church held their event, with St Just Church, at the rectory, opposite the lych-gate. This was called St Just fête, and we used to walk up in the afternoon and back home in the evening. It was usually dark when we came up the narrow lane through the farm to the main road. I remember one occasion there was a lot of rustling in the hedge and we all ran. It turned out to be a cow that had got out of the field.

A big event as far as the children were concerned was the arrival of a collier. This was either a two- or three-masted sailing ship that tied up at the outside part of the quay, as it was too deep to get to the inside berth. The ship had sailed around Lands End with coal from South Wales.

The coal was shovelled into wicker baskets by two men in the hold. Each basket was then hoisted up by the ship's winch and derrick and tipped into a horse-drawn cart on the quay. When the cart was full it went off along the quay, past the Ship & Castle hotel and the garage, then turned left up the back lane by Beach House. Here, at the back of the coal store, was a wooden covering which had been removed, giving access to the store below. The cart was reversed above this opening and the coal cascaded down into the store. There were two men inside the store continuously shovelling coal to one side. Three horses and carts were employed on the operation. In all it took about four days to empty the collier and by that time the quay and front were covered in coal dust and the road plastered with horse droppings.

There was a man known to me as Captain Pollard. He had an old Brixham trawler and used to take people out. He was a big man with a bushy black beard, who always went in the carnival as Black Beard the pirate. He lived up on the Rope Walk and his wife was a granddaughter to Gladstone, the old Prime Minister. When they wanted to have the old doors on the holy well done up she paid for the work to be done.

Donald Pollard

Harry Harris

When I was kid I can remember that a lot of the old pilchard gear was still in the cellars. Mr Hancock's seine was still in the loft. Up over the cellars in the

A view of St Mawes in the e,arly 1960s showing the St Mawes Café and the cake shop.

front street there were a lot of stores, all partitioned off with wire netting. This is where the fishermen kept their gear. It's all been made into flats now, with shops underneath.

Mrs Pomery used to own the garage down on the front and she would never be there. And so every time the boss would say to me, 'You better get some petrol for the van before you go out on the round,' I would have to go along the street and knock on her door and get her to open up the garage and she would never be in any hurry. 'Yes, yes, I won't be long, I will be along in a minute.' And by the time she opened up all the doors and you finally got your petrol you were late starting the round.

She had an old hard-tyred bus which used to go to Truro. Will Andrews was the driver and when there were several people on board the old bus would be struggling a bit. Many's the time we got to the bottom of Mill Hill and Will would shout,

'Everybody off, there's too much weight, you will have to walk up!' Before that old Ned Dotson used to have a cab.

Burt Truscott was the ploughman at Newton. We used two blacksmiths in those days. There was Mr Watts down Polvarth and Mr Palmer up St Just. I remember Cyril Green learning his trade as a blacksmith down Polvarth, and then later, when Palmer gave up the forge in St Just, Cyril took it over. I worked on the farm at Newton but when the second war started I was sent down to the butcher's shop, which also belonged to Mr Hancock. The shop was next to the St Mawes hotel. We opened three day a week in those days, as meat, like everything else, was rationed. We killed all our own stuff at the killing house, just above where the castle-keeper's house is.

Mrs Andrew, she ordered a goose from old boss Hancock, it was a very difficult time of year but he managed to get one. It had been grass fed and they taste a bit gamey like that. Anyway, she took this

The storms of 1963 caused a good deal of flooding and damage.

goose home and cooked it, and sliced off a piece. 'Ay,' she said, 'we can't eat that,' and she brought this cooked goose back down to the butcher's shop, which was about 100 yards down the road. 'We can't eat this, John Hancock,' she said. 'Well, my handsome, we will,' said boss, and we cut 'un up right there in the shop and ate the lot.

Harry Moon used to make baskets up St Just. There were a lot of withy gardens around then and he made all sorts of baskets for the various tradespeople. We used to go up there and collect these square baskets for carrying the meat in. Just up the road, on the other side from Dickie's yard, there used to be an old chap called Jack Shrub, who would break in a pony or a horse for anyone. All the ponies that were used in the traps and carts all had to be broken in, and this old chap lived there beside the road in an old tin hut with a settee in it.

Dickie Cocking

Old Ned Dotson used to deliver the coal with a pony and cart. He was a hard old nut, well you had to be in they days. His coal store was down on the corner opposite the Watch House. I can remember the old coal boats coming in. They would unload part of the load here and then they would take the rest up Percuil.

Charlie Dash, he used to have a donkey and cart, and used to go around picking up parcels and luggage to put on the steamer. There were a pile of donkeys around then, you could buy one or a pony off the moor for five bob.

When we needed building materials we used to row over to Falmouth in the *Lurker* and pick them up, say 6cwt cement and a load of timber, and then row back to St Mawes again.

Old Joe Dotson used to stand outside his front door in the evenings smoking his pipe. I used to see him there when I came home from courting.

Tommy Williams, he had an old donkey and a cart to get around in, the poor old chap had a gammy leg. I used to sing in the church choir with him.

Cyril Johns

There used to be a cobbler's shop over where the dairy is now. Sid Coe was the cobbler then. An old man called Clemo used to live next door. He had a gramophone with a big brass trumpet on it. I used to go down St Mawes from Gerrans delivering bread with old Jack Lett, with a horse and cart for Quintrell's bakery. That was when I was eight years old. Back then there were about five houses out what they now call New Road, the rest was just fields. We used to come down and deliver along the front and then up Church Hill.

Old Ned Dotson used to have a hearse but a lot of people couldn't afford it in those days. I remember when my uncle was drowned over in Falmouth

Nelly Green in 1961.

harbour, four men carried the coffin out of the house, and after about 100 yards, four other men took over. This went on all the way to St Just churchyard. There were that many men there to help that it wasn't until we got to the church that the four men who carried the coffin out of the house, took over and carried it into the church.

Douglas Sawle

Where the supermarket is now that was the coal store for the St Mawes Steam Ship Co. Before that all those building along there were net stores and fish cellars. At the other end was Joe Dotson's coal store – he worked for the St Mawes shareholders.

Halfway along the street there was a wall. The man that owned it was called Mr Step. In the wall there was a door which was kept locked if he wasn't

there. My father told me that when he was young if the door was locked they would climb around the end of the wall and go through, but if he caught them he would rap their fingers with a stick.

You will hear people say that that wall was separating the manors of St Mawes and Bohella, but that wasn't what it was for, it was a private key.

The King's Road, I think, was made in 1905. The road wasn't named after our king. Old Edwin Hicks, he was a builder, he built the Manor House and he was always known as the King of St Mawes. Anyway, the boundary of St Mawes and Bohelia was a stream which came down through the withy gardens, where the car park is now behind the Rising Sun.

I was born in one of the little cottages down by the slipway next to the Idle Rocks Hotel, so I was born in Bohella, not St Mawes.

Now old Fred Pascoe, he was my father's great-uncle. They came down to Polvarth from St Just Bar and had a boatbuilding business there. He was there until 1935.

Stone Works Quay is so called because that's where they unloaded the stone from Porthallow. Some of it was crushed there and some was taken away. They had an old steam engine down there and they had a railway track down to Bucky's Lane. They used the stone for road building.

The Rope Walk is where they made ropes. The family were called Hitchens, they came from North Cornwall. Old Harry Moon, the basket-maker, he used to live up St Austell Row. It was just a little one up and one down. When he had cut a load of withies from the withy garden down behind the Rising Sun he would lay them in his stairs – it was the only place he had that was long enough to put them.

The old carpenter's shop in Back Lane, that's where Frank Green used to work. He took it over from old Mr Barnicoat. The floor was so bad it used to go up and down, I don't know how they used to manage to work in there. He always had a lot of apprentices on at the same time. My father served his time with him. They used to start at 7 o'clock in the morning. They had to make a four-panelled door in a day, all from rough-sawn timber. Gaylards, the grocery people from over Gerrans, they had a shop here on the front.

There was a man down here called John Henry Andain. He was a chemist and he used to take photos on glass plates of old St Mawes. Years later, when Burt Sawle had the St Mawes Hotel, he found a lot of these old photographic plates put out for the dustbin men and he rescued them and had a lot of them taken off.

The Hancock family, they had a seine boat called *Onward*. I can remember there was a old black-smith's shop down Polvarth, and when I was a child there was two old seine boats laid up in there.

I served my apprenticeship with Frank Green, of

Staff at the Manor House Hotel, 1964. From left to right: *Jean Woodford, Ivor Tiddy, Mavis Tiddy, Simone (head waitress), Helen Tiddy.*

Green & Harris. He had a seine boat, she drifted away from somewhere and came ashore in St Mawes. He got her repaired and we used to use her to go to Falmouth to pick up timber.

Jimmy Lelean

You forget how hard people worked in the old days. I can remember Ellen Dotson carrying her wet washing from Grove Cottage up the hill to the Ropewalk to dry it at her mother's. They only had a very small back yard, with no room for hanging up clothes, so she would hang them up in her mother's garden. That was on Mondays, they always washed on Mondays.

The thatched cottage above Tavern Beach, that's where the Step family lived. Edward Step, he wrote a lot of books about nature.

Kim Chenoweth

When Roger and I lived in the little cottage on Marine Parade called Lys Vean, we had a ghost. He was dressed like an old fisherman would have dressed many years ago. He always sat in the same place and seemed to be waiting for someone to return

to the cottage. Maybe he was not able to go out fishing anymore and was waiting for the others to return safely.

In Memory of Frankie Peters

That St Mawes has become one of the best known and most frequented holiday resorts on the south coast of Cornwall, was in many was inevitable. Its mostly sheltered position, its beautiful coastal walks and its almost continental appearance, all go to make it stand out against many other villages on this coast.

In 1957 *The Lady* carried a report on the wonders of St Mawes and brought to the nation's attention local boatbuilder Frankie Peter.

The place is small, but has four very good Hotels and several runners up. It is quiet, but a well sophisticated quietness, that means the visitors are playing Canasta in their rooms, not going early to bed. The paradox of St Mawes is that, for all its chic, it remains a family resort. The people I see wandering round the harbour at night, having a coffee in the minute coffee bar, or a drink in the Victory Inn, kept by Capt. Miners, a retired square rig master, are parents holidaying with their young children.

The Idle Rocks Hotel

When the school holidays started, the harbour filled with small sailing craft, each with a crew of sunburnt children. Their hero is Frankie Peters, a local boat builder, whose sailing skill is unbeatable. Mr Moseley has acquired eighteen properties in St Mawes over the last ten years. These include the two hotels, Idle Rocks and the Ship & Castle, various cottages which are used as annexes and his own beautiful late Georgian house on the hill.

Boatbuilding had long been an important trade at St Mawes. This industry was centred around Polvarth. As well as boats for the river and inshore trade, some substantial craft were built. The 14 ton sloop *Active* was built in 1786 and the following year the slightly larger *Friendship*. Out of 14 vessels listed between 1786 and 1832, the 186 ton barque *Duke of Kent*, built in 1806, is the largest vessel to be built at Polvarth.

Frank Peters was born on 2 September 1902. The Peters family has long been associated with the boatbuilding trade in St Mawes. The family had run their yard at Freshwater for over 200 years. The firm were responsible for building most of the original pilot gigs used so extensively, particularly around the Isles of Scilly. They also built gigs for Lloyds, the insurance company, and for the Coastguard preventive service. Records show that many preventive service stations were equipped with either a four- or six-oared gig. Portscatho, for example, had both a four-

and a six-oared gig, both equipped with oars and a lugsail main and mizzen. Both these boats were built at Freshwater by the Peters family. In 1872 the Portscatho station ordered a new four-oared gig from William Peters and in the same month he is recorded as having repaired 'the Gerrans boat'.

The timber used in the construction of these gigs was narrow or small-leaf Cornish elm. The tree trunks selected had to be of sufficient length to provide planks of 30ft. Only one scarf joint would be used in any one plank. The trunks were floated up to Freshwater and submerged in the mud, using heavy chains, for up to five years. After this period of seasoning, they were hauled to shore and placed over the saw pit. The 'sawyer' was a man from Penryn, who travelled in a hand-operated paddle boat. According to R.H.C. Gillis, the saw could cut through a trunk as much as one foot per stroke. In those early days it is rumoured that the Peters' saw pit was also used on Sundays for cock fighting.

When the St Mawes Sailing Club was formed in 1920, racing was always in handicap starts because of the disparities between the boats taking part. Frank Peters then raced the 14ft clinker dinghy *White Duck*, which had been left at his boatyard by three Army officers stationed at St Anthony during the First World War. He was, however, often beaten by Dr James, a GP from Restronguet, in his William Ferris-built 16-footer *Phantom*.

In the early 1920s St Mawes already had a one-design class which had been designed by Frank Green. Only four of the class were built, and due to some skulduggery within the fleet, several owners sold their boats and interest dwindled. This was an opportune moment for Frankie, and the defeats by the *Phantom* led to him designing a boat with which he could win races. His design took over from the Green design and was formally adopted by the St Mawes Sailing Club. This boat was named *Aileen* and became the forerunner of the class.

Launched in 1923, she was of carvel construction with pine planking on ribs of rock elm. To give the boat stability, six 56lb weights were incorporated into the design, together with a cast-iron centreplate weighing 150lbs. She was gunter rigged, both her mast and yard being of hollow bamboo. She won the Falmouth Town Regatta class for 16ft dinghies three years in a row – 1923\24\25 – proving that Frankie was a talented 21-year-old boat builder and sailor. Through the twenties and thirties he built a further 13 boats, although no more than two per year were ever built. They took approximately six weeks to construct.

Keen competitive racing started again as soon as the war finished, and the fleet was enhanced by the addition of six more boats, built by Frankie between 1949 and 1951.

Frankie owned the *Aileen* from 1923 until 1949, when she was sold for £150 to John Mills on his return from the war, having been away for six years. The *Aileen* was bought by John mainly to acquire the Seagull outboard, a rare and valuable asset after the war. The Seagull eventually met its demise over the side. With the Mills family living in Kensington, the *Aileen* was eventually taken to Chichester harbour, where, renamed *Pigeon*, she was kept at Del Quay Sailing Club. In 1974 she was given to the Goldwyn family and moved to Twickenham, and sailed for many years on the Thames. She was thought to have been lost until 1987, but was spotted in a front garden in Thames Ditton from the top of a double-decker bus. She was found in virtually original condition, even with her original bamboo spars. She was brought back to St Mawes and restored by Jonathan Leach to her original specification.

Even in his late seventies Frankie was frequently seen in his bass boat following the racing, and would offer a tow home to one-design and Sunbeam sailors if the wind was light.

On New Year's Day 1990 she was relaunched in the presence of Frankie Peters at Freshwater Boat Yard. On 24 August 2003 the *Aileen* was sailed to the National Maritime Museum, where she is now on loan.

On 11 June 1995 William Francis Peters, or Frankie, as he was better known, the Class Association Commodore, designer and builder of 24 boats, passed away. After a moving service at St Mawes Methodist Church, he was laid to rest in St Just churchyard. His coffin was carried with great pride by two teams of bearers, all one-design sailors past and present, including Miles Carden, Mark Cocking, Stefan Green, Andrew Curtis, Gary Hitchings, Jonathan Leach, Glen Litherland and Andy Tyler.

The Poet Laureate John Betjeman, on visiting St Mawes, wrote: 'Because there is no railway and the distance by ferry from Falmouth is considerable there is not much Victorian building.'

He did, however, go on to say that there had been quite a large expansion since the 1930s:

Later development came with the motor age. The nineteen thirties filled the gaps between the Georgian houses with villas, creating a new estate at the top of the Town which gave the place its character for dignified and opulent retired people, which it still maintains. Bronzed and wearing panama hats, and old grey flannels and tweed jackets, they may be seen walking along the front. Comfortable hotels cater for their children and grandchildren in their holidays. There is, of course, the inevitable complement of yachtsmen.

CHAPTER 16

St Mawes AFC

In days gone by St. Mawes AFC's unofficial club-house was the St Mawes Hotel. Here teams were picked, goals were scored and wins and losses were discussed.

St Mawes AFC
by A J Morris

The St Mawes AFC is a wonderful Club,
Though most of their training is done in the pub,
For the last fifty years they've played with stout hearts,
But when they play Gerrans they play just like farts.
Now that was a very unkind thing to say,
St Mawes can beat Gerrans just any old day,
Please don't take any notice of idle abuse,
It's not meant to injure, but just to amuse.
I've followed the fortunes of this village Club,
I've watched all their games from my seat in the pub,
They've played some fine games, but the best ones by far,
Are the ones that I've heard played right here in the bar.
The Club's full of characters, some old and some young,
Some work with the ball and some with the tongue,
The players all try hard you have to admit,
Though at times, let's be honest, they get on your tits.
The selection committee no doubt are to blame,
I wonder they don't hang their heads down in shame,
When the Secretary pins the team on the board
Friday night,

All the critics flock around him filled with delight.

For a moment all is silence and then with a shout,
Sawly says 'Strike me crimson, they've left Bazer out!
Then up comes Billy Mitchell and says with a grunt,
'Jeffrey Hitchens Left wing? Huh! Might as well pick
Joe Hunt.'
You see our dear Willie, it's sad to relate,
Can only remember the year 28,
When discussing present day teams he's been heard to
say
'Buggers don't know their right from their left leg
today.'
But why Bazer's left out no one can understand,
'Cos in spite of his age he's the best of the band,
Till George Preston comes in with a hell of a rush,
Bazer's in isolations, they think he's got Thrush.
This causes consternation and makes the boys think,
Which is good biz for Sawly as they all buy more drink,
The boys all stand around, they are looking quite vague,
Till Jimmy Austin says to Tatie, 'Go fetch Henry
Teague.'
Then in comes our Henry looking downcast and glum
Saying, 'Gis a glass a cider, Ronnie and chuck in some
Rum.'
'Now boys,' says our Henry, 'If you want my advice
You'll send right away for Trice Thomas the Vice.'

Undated photo of the St Mawes team.

Mr Thomas came quickly, we all knew he would,
He always was ready to help if he could,
But on hearing the news and still suffering from shock,
Said, 'Tis too big for me boys, send for John Hancock.

Then in came the President looking serious and wise,
He'd heard the bad news, you could tell by his eyes,
He said, 'Now then you fellows, 'tis no good to mope,
I've heard Bazer's still talking, so there must be some
hope.'
Since then Bazer's come home and is looking quite well,
But it just goes to show, you never can tell.
The committee, what troubles they face
Chasing players all over the place.
They pick a good team, they think it's first class,
Then it's John Preston can't play, got a boil on his ass.
Bruce Cocking and Patrick are gone Rock'n'Roll,
You can't have Al Morris, he's stuck on the Toll.
Hughie's courting, Pussy's working, Oh dearie me,
You can't have John Andrew, he's watching TV.
Dennis can't play, he's home minding the twins,
No use asking Basil, he's weak on his pins.
Brian Edwards can't play, he's up Joe's playing crib,
Jimmy Thomas is out, bust his leg or his rib.
Graham Hancock won't be there, got a date with a cow,
Artificial Insemination, it's all the rage now!
Ronnie Tiddy and Bert Green suspended, can't put
them in,
Ungentlemanly conduct, they drank too much Gin!
Jimmy Benny's gone Plymouth with Willum by car,
Richard Mitchell's gone too, what a fine bunch they are.

Chris Mitchell, I'm afraid, won't be with us today,
'Cos up Waterloo they've a cow gone to lay.
Mike Hearn is gone fishing, I think it's a sin,
He'll bring back some Pollock if he don't fall in,
Charlie Ferris, our trainer, is in a bad way;
He's mislaid his sponge, so he's out for today.
Charlie Green is quite willing, I expect he'll be there,
Looking his age with his pate of white hair.
Walt Hitchens, he's had it, if you ask him he'll say
'Better go up St Just and dig up some of they.'
Tommy Andrew's signed on, let's give him a go,
No! on second thoughts he's too ruddy slow,
He's young and at times he cavorts quite nimbly,
Yet it took him four days to sweep Oony's chimney.
It's a hell of a thing when you can't find a team
In a place like St Mawes it's just like a dream.
But let's face it boys, we ain't got no hope,
'Cos all we got left now is Barrer Boy Cope!
Then young Warren Austin says, 'Please can I play?'
And Shushi and Dominic they'll both play today.
Then there's Lala and Lennie and Winnie the Pooh,
And if that's not enough I can get Lardy too.
We'll play like the devil, you've got nothing to fear,
If you pick us we'll play for the rest of the year.

We'll win you the League and the Lockhart Cup too,
Show St Mawes what the youngsters can do.
Poor Henry just sits there, head held on high,
Don't know if he should laugh or if he should cry.
And then for the first time in full fifty years
He Shouts, 'Cancel the Match' and dissolves into tears.

The St Mawes team. Players and coaches include G. Preston, Bert Hamling, W. Kendall, J. Thomas, Bazar Hitchens, B. Edwards, Charlie Green; Mr Green, Charlie Sawle, C. Green, Stanley Ferris.

St Mawes

St Mawes

❖ CHAPTER 17 ❖

A Continental Air

By the early 1960s a remarkable ex-diplomat turned hotelier had well and truly put St Mawes on the tourist map.

It was at this time that the village gained its almost continental air. It was reported in 1965 that Mr Harley Moseley was employing 100 foreign workers, including Spanish, Italians, French, Greeks, Swiss and Austrians.

Mr Moseley, who lived in the Regency period house 'Braganza', had first come to the village on honeymoon 20 years before.

Within six months he had acquired his first hotel. By 1965 his estate boasted 20 buildings and 250 beds.

Throughout the First World War he had served in the American Army, and was the only junior officer allowed to forge General Pershing's signature. While stationed in Paris he hunted out the best restaurants and arranged the dinners for the General Staff. His appointment as ADC was the stepping-stone to the American Foreign Service, working in Paris, India and Australia.

Mrs Moseley was also no stranger to the limelight. As the poet Zofia Elinska, she had left her native Poland to attend Reading University. She went on to publish a Polish translation of T.S. Eliot's *Murder in the Cathedral*.

On 26 November 1971, large-scale improvements at St Mawes were announced:

There is great activity on the sea front at St Mawes as contractors widen the coastal road in the £200,000 sewerage scheme undertaken by the Rural District Council, in order that one of the two pumping stations may be built underground. The scheme, which is expected to be finished in July 1973, will mean that further expansion in St Mawes will be possible. It will also mean that the beaches in St Mawes creek will no longer be polluted by discharged overflow.

1972:

The yachtsman's haven of St Mawes emerged battered, bruised and flooded as South Cornwall's worst hit storm spot yesterday, after taking the full fury of the early morning's howling southerly gale. At the height of the force 9, rising to 10 gales, giant waves broke clean over the Idle Rocks Hotel, probably the village's worst hit property, and other waterfront buildings.

Practically all harbourside premises were flooded, many of them also from the landward side by waves flung over their roofs. Throughout yesterday, with the wind still blowing strongly and the forecast threatening more gales; workmen were fighting a battle against the clock, to shore-up a damaged section of seawall in time to prevent further damage by the evening's high tide. Timber, ladders and other equipment being used in new sewage installations were washed away or found strewn about the beach.

The powerful waves, driven by the high winds, disturbed the seawall in front of the Idle Rocks Hotel's wide windowed dining-room, dislodging heavy granite blocks. One section of window was broken and its frame pushed away from the wall into the room. Mr Bert Hitchings, foreman for maintenance at the hotel, said it was the worst gale he had seen for ten years. His big worry, as he surveyed sodden carpets, was whether the seawall workmen would succeed in time, or whether more windows would break, causing further flooding and damage.

The hotel's lounge, like other buildings, was flooded by clean over-the-top waves, which burst in through the back doors. Another part of the hotel complex, the seafront Buttery, was flooded to a depth, in places, of four to six inches. But damage to St Mawes could have been much worse, residents said, if they had not learnt their lesson from the disastrous gale of 1962. St Mawes chemist Mr John Gerry said he had learnt his lesson in 1962 and, through putting up his shutters, had only minor flooding.

Mr Thomas and party,.c.1930.

The regatta carnival, c.1930.

✤ CHAPTER 18 ✤

St Mawes Regatta

Like so many other Cornish fishing villages, St Mawes has held an annual regatta for many, many years. When it first took place is very hard to say. It was only with the advent of the local newspapers that such events were recorded.

An article published in 1861 concerning a regatta which was held at St Mawes states that:

The spectators at St Mawes were very numerous; the quay and famous sea wall in front of the town being crowded with hundreds of interested sightseers. Emidy, with his well known band, was stationed on an elevated platform and performed interesting marches, waltzes and other music; and there were also the energetic performances of a volunteer juvenile band.

The town was gaily decorated with flags and evergreens and, to those who have visited the picturesque town of St Mawes; it was needless to say more. Those who have not, will do well to go to the next year's regatta.

Everything connected with it, passed off well. And, much to the credit of the committee, to whom the public are indebted for a day's holiday and a good day's sport. And many there, on departing, said they would not be far off when the next regatta took place.

At the close of the regatta, some amusing games were enjoyed to the entire satisfaction of the juveniles, such as climbing a pole for a leg of mutton, diving for apples and other diversions, and afterwards, a display of fireworks took place.

That report was nearly 150 years ago, and I am happy to report that the St Mawes regatta is still going strong and is a day not to be missed.

Among the local ladies pictured here are Maud Lelean, Ena Watts and Muriel Dotson.

Regatta float, c.1940.

The regatta in 1959.

Janet Gay, aged 3, enters the carnival helped by her grandmother, Ella Bryant, in 1954.

Winter 1962/63 saw the water in the harbour frozen.

In the 1960s Fisher's café was a popular place for the young people of the village to hang out.

Jillian Austin and Douglas Clode, 1964.

Phil Tucker, Trevor Hitchins, Louise Fisher, Jillian Austin and Diana Sawle, 1965.

Left: *Jillian Austin, Louise Fisher, Diana Sawle, Trevor Hitchins and Philip Tucker, 1964.*

Trevor Green, Jackie Harris, Charlie Ferris, Louise Fisher, Ricky Iddison, Trevor Hitchins and Cherry Mathews, 1967.

The pride of St Mawes – Jackie Tiddy, Diana Sawle, Jillian Austin, Louise Fisher, Teresa Tiddy and Cherry Fisher, 1964

St Mawes Carnival Queen Valerie Gaye and attendants Sandra Harris and Michelle Sawle, 1965.

Looking cool, Jackie Harris, Trevor Hitchins and local harmonica player Phil Tucker, 1966.

Enjoying the bar at the Ship & Castle, Jackie Harris, Chris Pollard, Janet Gay and Angie, 1968.

Sonny Bryant, well known for his participation in putting on local shows, here performs at the Ship & Castle Hotel with his black and white minstrels in the 1960s.

The St Mawes Players, 1967. Left to right, back row: *Diana Sawle, Ann Miners, Trevor Hitchins, Theresa Tiddy, Sonny Bryant, Margaret Kent, Eleanor Preston, Loretta Tiddy, Butch Gay, Judith Tiddy, ?; front row: Janet Gay, Louise Fisher, Michelle Sawle, Jillian Austin, Sandra Harris, Jeanette Harris.*

Louise Fisher sitting outside her parents' restaurant on Marine Parade in 1967.

Cherry Fisher shows off her pride and joy to Mary Bryson, 1972.

Top and above: *The Queen Mother arrives at St Mawes in 1969 to be greeted by an excited crowd.*

The Queen's visit to St Mawes on 6 August 1977 as part of her silver jubilee celebrations. In the photo below are Muriel Dotson and Keith and Janet Ferris.

Above and below: *St Mawes girl pipers in the 1970s. Belinda Gay is in the centre of picture.*

The gig William Peters on her launching day at Freshwater, which attracted a large crowd in May 1987.

Carnival time with (left to right, back row) *Robert Cope, Trevor Hitchins, ?, ?, ?, Sonny Bryant;* front row: *Megan Gay, Belinda Austin Butch Gay.*

In the 1980s St Mawes held its annual trawler race.

Bill Brown and Howard Lees at St Mawes Sailing Club in the mid-1980s.

Top and above: *There was no shortage of snow in St Mawes in the winter of 1987.*

St Just in Roseland churchyard and Pasco's boatyard were badly damaged by hurricane-force winds in 1987.

St Just in Roseland churchyard, damaged by hurricane-force winds in 1987.

Kym Ferris and Natasha Green in Cinderella, *1990.*

Shirley Curtis wearing fruit hat and Kym Ferris (centre) stage at St Mawes Memorial Hall, 1992, with Diana Grey, Rachael Chenoweth and Pauline Hurcombe.

Butch and Megan Gay, dressed for the carnival, 1990.

Local fisherman Peter Green, a member of one of the oldest fishing families in St Mawes, 2006.

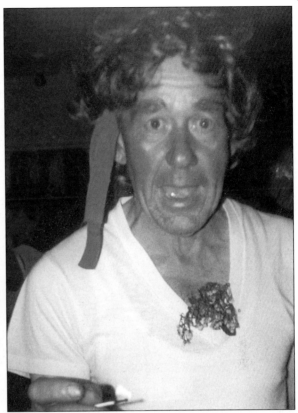

Sonny Bryant preparing to dance around the maypole, 1988.

Sonny later that evening.

Belinda Austin and Janet Pollard, 1991.

Dancing around the maypole, 1988.

Meals on wheels St Mawes style, 1986.

St Mawes' own fairy godmother, Hilary Austin, appearing in Jack and the Beanstalk in 1991.

Traditional stargazy pie served up by landlady Debbie with Rob with staff member Urik in the background, 2006.

The fish festival, 2006.

Tony Tomlinson, Dave Cannon and Geoff Tomlinson preparing scallops at the fish festival.

The working boats racing for the Victory Cup, 2006.

St Mawes

✦ CHAPTER 19 ✦

Epilogue

And so the soldiers are consigned to the history books, the fish cellars demolished to make way for flats and shops and the seine boats have been replaced by luxury yachts, but the heart of St Mawes beats on.

The village school still opens its doors each weekday to the throng of infants and juniors. There is a low-cost housing programme now in operation to see that young local families are not driven out of the village by inflated house prices.

The sailing club, with its clubhouse overlooking the harbour, keeps up a busy schedule, with racing throughout the summer months and, of course, the ever popular regatta. In 2006 St Mawes hosted its first Fish Festival, which was hailed a great success. The bustling hotels cater for the tourist's every need, as do the waterfront bars. What could be nicer than sitting and chatting in the Victory, the only original inn left in the village. Or, if your tastes are more modern, you will find plenty of room at the Tresanton Hotel, the Rising Sun, the Ship & Castle, the St Mawes Hotel, the Watch House or the Idle Rocks. If it's a game of snooker you're after, then pop into the club. Or if you are fit and able, become a member of the Gig Club.

These days in St Mawes you can purchase almost anything your heart desires, from groceries to trinkets to antiques to works of art – the list is endless. But at the base of all this are the people of St Mawes. With some families going back hundreds of years there is still a strong sense of community, and new blood must not be forgotten or ignored. The village has always been a place to which people have gravitated for a variety of reasons. And so this remote little corner of Britain can be proud of its history and of its achievements, and we look forward to the coming years with great enthusiasm.

Books and Newspapers Consulted
Roseland Heritage Coast Historic Audit
Kelly's Directory, 1873
The Falmouth Packets, Tony Pawlyn
Passenger Steamers of the River Fal, Alan Kittridge
Cornwall, John Betjeman
Wreck and Rescue Round the Cornish Coast, Cyril Noall and Grahame Farr
The Saints of Cornwall, Gilbert H. Doble
Pendennis and St Mawes, S. Pasfield Oliver
The West Briton
The Falmouth Packet
The Cornish Echo
The Lady

ST. MAWES PIER AND HARBOUR CO.

with

ST. JUST IN ROSELAND PARISH COUNCIL

ADMIT

M^{iss} Dotsoly

to St. Mawes Pier

on the occasion of the visit of
HER MAJESTY THE QUEEN
on
SATURDAY, AUGUST 6th, 1977
from 2.45 p.m.

No Admission after 3.45 p.m.   Signed ....

Subscribers

Jane Andain, Gerrans, Cornwall

Ian Andrew, Falmouth, Cornwall

Neil Andrew, Falmouth, Cornwall

Harry Andrew, Wellington, Somerset

Dawn Andrews, St Mawes

Alan Atherton, Runcorn, Cheshire

Richard J. Atkins, Harpenden, Herts

Suzanne Ball (née Green), Dobwalls

Mrs K. Bellman (née Drinkwater)

Jim and Suzanne Benney, St Mawes, Cornwall

Chris Bickle, Crowtrees Farm, Oakamoor, Staffordshire

J.P.H. Blackie, Auchterarder, Scotland

Mr Paul & Mrs Michelle Borrie and Family, Gerrans, Cornwall

John G. Bryant, St Mawes, Cornwall

Trevor Bryant

Trystan Bryant

K. J. Burrow, Bucks Cross, Devon

Robert D. Clifford-Wing, Philleigh

William Charles (Charlie) Collins, Plymouth, Devon

Ann Cragg, St Mawes, Cornwall

Will Crewes, St Mawes

Laura and Martin Davies, Upper Castle Road, St Mawes, Cornwall

Joy Day, St Mawes, Cornwall

Chris De Glanville, St Mawes

Natasha de Kergorlay, Braganza, St Mawes

Mr and Mrs P.R.K. Fender

Virginia Field, St Mawes

Sean. J. Finnegan, Gerryns, Cornwall

Lt. Col. and Mrs John Garnett, St Just-in-Roseland

Andrew and Elizabeth German, Grampound Road, Cornwall

Richard and Keelin German, Monkstown, Dublin

Ralph and Lesley German, St Just-in-Roseland, Cornwall

Julian and Maria German, Scarcewater, Cornwall

Peter John Green, St Mawes

David Green, St Mawes, Cornwall

Chris Greet, Walton-on-Thames, Surrey

Teresa Hansen-Pollard

Mark and Susanne Hatwood, Portscatho

Malcom Hay, St Mawes, Cornwall

Ivy M. Hearn, St Mawes, Cornwall

Mr and Mrs J.W. Hender

Mr and Mrs M.J. Hender

Mr C.J. Hender

Mr and Mrs N.J. Hender

J. Hillier, Farncombe, Surrey

Vanessa and Martin Hoare, Ashtead, Surrey

John R. Horton, St Mawes, Cornwall

Alan January, St Mawes

Philip Johnstone, Box 13, Lake Cowichan, BC, Canada V0R 2G0

Marlene Kavanagh, Parkville, Victoria, Australia

Jonathan Leach, St Mawes

Nicholas Leach, St Mawes

Peter E. Leach, F.S.A., St Mawes

Kathleen Lyndon (née Dennis), Probus

Martin and Diana McCarthy, West Wickham, Kent

Derek and Linda McKeown, St Just-in-Roseland, Cornwall

Mrs Kay E. Medlyn, Camborne

Peter Messer-Bennetts, Portscatho

R.J. And B. Morse

Krysia Moseley-Kergorlay, Braganza, St Mawes

Elizabeth and Jerome O'Hea, St Mawes

John and June O'Leary, St Mawes, Cornwall

Mary Alice Pollard

Rod Remnant-Ashton, Fareham, Hants

Tessa Rice (née Andrew), Hanham, Bristol

Rodney T. Roberts, St Mawes

William N. Roberts, St Agnes, Cornwall

Mr Michael Rosewall, St Mawes

Mr Keith John Rosewall, St Just-in-Roseland

Mr John F. Ryder, Sparry Lane, Carharrack, Cornwall

Phil Salter, St Mawes

Mrs Diana Sanderson, Mawnan Smith, Cornwall

Mr David Sanderson, Mawnan Smith, Cornwall

Francis and Shirley Sawle, Hythe, Southampton

Doris Sawle, Lee-on-the-Solent, Hampshire

Natalie Sawle, Dibden Purlieu, Southampton

Claire Sawle, Marchwood, Southampton

Marilyn Skelton (née Collins), Avonwick, Devon

Christopher and Margaret Skidmore, Idle Rocks Hotel

Thora Southeard (née Hitchings), St Mawes, Cornwall

Mrs Spry-Grant-Dalton, Place, Cornwall

Major A. T. Stephenson, St Mawes, Cornwall

Mr and Mrs P. Swait, Gerrans, Cornwall

John and Judy Taylor, St Mawes

Peter Teague, Harbour View, St Just-in-Roseland

Dave and Bobbie, The Royal Standard, Gerrans

Graham Thorne, Maldon

Michael and Pauline Tregellas, Solihull, West Midlands

R.J. Truscott, Truro, Cornwall

Philip Van Grutten

Paul M. J. Vincent, St Mawes, Cornwall

Dr J. B. Walker, Quay House, Portscatho

K and S Walker, St Mawes

John F.W. Walling, Newton Abbot, Devon

Croyden and Miriam Whittaker, St Mawes

C.N. Wiblin, St Levan, Cornwall

G.J.K. Widgery, Little Lodge, St Mawes

Ian and Alex Wood, Bakewell, Derbyshire

David and Patricia Yorke, St Mawes